William Blades

A List of Medals, Jettons, Tokens, etc.

In Connection with Printers and the Art of Printing

William Blades

A List of Medals, Jettons, Tokens, etc.
In Connection with Printers and the Art of Printing

ISBN/EAN: 9783337251154

Printed in Europe, USA, Canada, Australia, Japan

Cover: Foto ©Andreas Hilbeck / pixelio.de

More available books at **www.hansebooks.com**

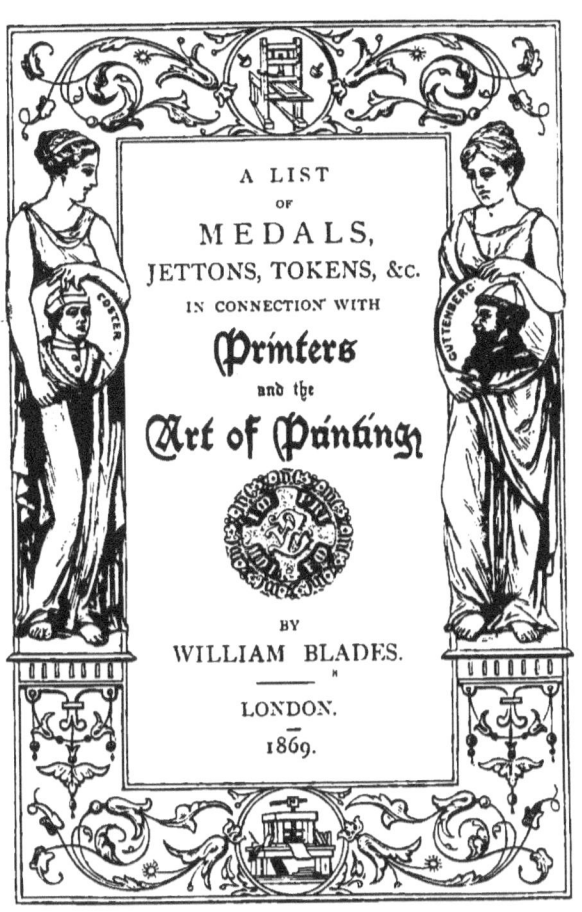

A LIST
OF
MEDALS,
JETTONS, TOKENS, &c.
IN CONNECTION WITH

Printers

and the

Art of Printing.

BY
WILLIAM BLADES.

LONDON.
1869.

This Edition consists of 100 *copies only, of which* 25 *are upon Fcap. 4to., and* 75 *upon Fcap. 8vo.*

Not printed for Sale.

TO THE READER.

THE present publication, purposely restricted to a bare description of each Medal, is intended as a forerunner of a similar work upon a more extended scale. Several reasons have induced me to publish thus prematurely, of which perhaps the chief is an ardent wish to redeem promises made long since to various kind friends and correspondents. Two years ago I thought a month or two would suffice to exhaust the subject; and little did I then anticipate the many pleasant walks in the bye-paths of lite-

AU LECTEUR.

CET opuscule limité, à dessein, à la simple description de chaque Médaille, n'a pour but que d'ouvrir la voie à un ouvrage semblable, mais sur une plus vaste échelle. J'ai été conduit à publier celui-ci prématurément par plusieurs raisons, dont la principale peut-être est un ardent désir de racheter des promesses faites depuis longtemps à nombre d'amis et de correspondants. Il y a deux ans, je m'imaginais pouvoir épuiser le sujet en un ou deux mois; et je ne prévoyais guère alors les nombreux détours agréables qui se trouvent dans les sentiers de la littérature, ni les labo-

rature, or the plodding research necessary, before the subject of *Printers' Medals* could be fully and accurately treated.

The materials already collected for this purpose will make a fair volume in Royal 8vo, to be entitled

NUMISMATA TYPOGRAPHICA

the plan of which will be found in a Prospectus inserted at the end of this volume.

Another reason for publishing now is the hope that the very imperfections of *this* list may tend to the greater perfection of that to come, by drawing attention to Medals at present untraceable or unknown.

Au Lecteur. ix

rieuses récherches indispensables, avant de pouvoir traiter complétement et avec exactitude le sujet des *Médailles typographiques*.

Les matériaux déja réunis dans ce but, formeront un fort volume, grand in-8, qui sera intitulé :

NUMISMATA TYPOGRAPHICA

et dont le plan se trouve dans un Prospectus inséré à la fin de ce volume.

Une autre raison pour faire cette publication anticipée est l'espoir que les imperfections mêmes de cette liste me permettront de combler les lacunes qui peuvent se trouver encore dans le grand ouvrage, en attirant l'attention sur les Médailles qui restent inconnues ou dont la trace est perdue.

x   *To the Reader.*

For much useful information and assistance I am indebted to friends and correspondents. I thank them most heartily, and hope to do so in a more particular and personal manner when the forthcoming *Numismata Typographica* shall appear. Special information has been given me by Mr. Alkan aîné, of Paris; MM. Clérot and Caignard, of the Musée des Monnaies, of the same city; Mr. Louis Mohr, of Strasbourg; Mr. Camile Picque, of the Royal Museum, Brussels; Mr. Pomba, of Turin; Mr. Jeronimo de Vries, of Amsterdam; and by the Messrs. Bom, booksellers, of the same city: to each and all of whom I tender my most hearty thanks. With-

Au Lecteur. xi

Je suis redevable de beaucoup de renseignements précieux à des amis et correspondants, que je remercie cordialement dès maintenant, tout en, me réservant de renouveler ces remerciements d'une manière plus personelle quand les *Numismata Typographica* paraîtront. J'ai reçu des renseignements speciaux de M. Alkan aîné, de Paris; MM. Clérot et Caignard, du Musée des Monnaies de la même ville ; de M. Louis Mohr, de Strasbourg ; de M. Camille Picque, du Musée Royal de Bruxelles ; de M. Pomba, de Turin ; de M. Jeronimo, de Vries d'Amsterdam ; et de MM. Bom, libraires, de la même ville ; à qui collectivement et individuellement, j'addresse mes remerciements sincères. Sans

out the generous aid of friends in many cities and towns, far apart, the simple list here given would have been an impossibility.

To make my next List as complete as possible is my ardent wish, and I therefore beg assistance from the reader. There *must* be many Medals and Jettons connected with Printing hitherto unnoticed, especially such as have been struck by local Associations for mutual help, by Benefit Societies, Printers' Guilds, and private Firms. Certain Festival Medals also, especially some of the 1740 Jubilee, have hitherto eluded my grasp. A list of these and others, wanted to complete my collection, will be printed at the

Au Lecteur. xiii

l'aide d'amis habitant des villes séparées par de grandes distances, il m'eut été impossible de dresser même la simple liste qui suit.

Je désire ardemment faire ma prochaine liste aussi complète que possible, et à ce titre je demande que mes lecteurs veuillent bien m'aider. Il *doit* y avoir beaucoup de Médailles et de Jettons relatifs à la Typographie, et qui n'ont pas été décrits ; surtout ceux qui ont été frappés par les Sociétés de participation, les Corporations d'Imprimeurs, et des Maisons particulières. Certaines Médailles de Jubilés anniversaires, particulierèment du Jubilé de 1740, m'ont échappé jusqu'ici. Une liste de celles-ci et d'autres, nécessaires pour compléter ma collection, sera

end of the volume under the heading "Desiderata."

Should the reader come across any such Medals, he will confer a lasting favour by addressing a letter to the Author, by whom any information will be fully acknowledged and thankfully received.

WILLIAM BLADES.

11, Abchurch Lane, London,
May, 1869.

imprimée à la fin du volume sous le titre de " Desiderata."

Si le lecteur trouvait par hasard quelques unes de ces Médailles, il rendrait à l'Auteur un service signalé, en lui adressant par écrit des renseignements qui seraient reçus avec reconnaissance.

WILLIAM BLADES.

LONDON,
ABCHURCH LANE, 11,
Mai, 1869.

A LIST OF PRINTERS'
MEDALS AND JETTONS.

ALDUS PIUS MANUTIUS.

Venice, c. 1500.

PLATE A.

Obverse.—The bust of Aldus to the left, with long hair and a cap upon his head. The surrounding legend is :—
ALDVS PIUS . MANVTIVS . R.

Reverse.—The well-known device used by Aldus in his books : an Anchor, around which is a Dolphin. The legend is : ΣΠΕΤΔΕ ΒΡΑΔΕΩΣ.

JOHN PETREIUS.

Nuremberg, 1545.

PLATE B.

Obverse.—The bust of Petreius to the right in professorial cap and fur collar. Around is the legend : IOH . PETREIVS . TYPOGRAPHVS . ANNO AET SVÆ IIL . ANNO 1545 :

Reverse.—A modification of the device used by Petreius in his books, viz.: a hand holding upright a flaming sword; on the left side of which are the letters I P. in a monogram. The surrounding legend is : SERMO DEI IGNITVS . ET PENETRANTIOR . QUOVIS . GLADIO . ANCIPITI.

PARIS. 1551.

PLATE C.

Obverse.—St. John the Evangelist, with a nimbus around his head, standing in the midst of the flames of his martyrdom, his right hand extended in the act of benediction, and his left holding the poisoned chalice, whence serpents issue. Upon the left side of the figure is the letter S, and upon the right the letter I.

Reverse.—A curved palm branch between two open books, with two clasps each. Above is the date 1551 in Arabic figures, part on one side, and part on the other, and beneath upon the left side of the branch is the letter S, and upon the right the letter I.

PARIS. 1569.

Plate D.

Obverse.—St. John the Evangelist with a nimbus around his head, standing upon two branches of palm, both arms extended, the left holding the poisoned chalice, whence serpents issue.

Reverse.—An imitation of the last, but without clasps to the books; the date 15 69, part on one side, and part on the other.

PARIS. 15- .

E (NO PLATE)

Obverse.—The same as the last.

Reverse.—An imitation of the last, but without date.

GEORGE BAUMAN.

Breslau, 1601.

PLATE F.

Obverse.—An unfinished building, upon which is a crane lifting up materials, and in front of which a " Builder" stands holding a square. The surrounding legend, between two beaded circles, is as follows:
·:· GEORG · BAWMAN . TYPOGRAPHVS . M.D.CI.

Reverse.—Within a double circle, beaded and ornamented, this inscription in five short lines : AVDI . VI . DE ET TACE . SI . VI . S . VI . VERE . IN . PACE.

MIDDLEBURG. 1631.

Plate G.

Obverse.—A rude wooden press with an inking ball on each side. The surrounding legend is : ✱ PAVLVS WANTE . EN IAN DE MEY ˙ BELED.

Reverse.—A binder's hand-press, upon which is an open book. Legend :—
✱ ZACHARIAS ˙ ˙ ROMAN, ˙ DEKEN ˙ 1631.

MIDDLEBURG. 1631.

Plate H.

Obverse.—The same as the Reverse of the last.

Reverse.—A funeral bier, over which is the mortuary cloth of the Guild. Legend: HEDEN . MY . MORGHEN . DY. A 1631 :

AMSTERDAM. 1639?

Plate I.

Obverse.—An old wooden printing-press in a room with two windows, the inking slab with a pair of balls to the left; a composing-case to the right. The surrounding legend is : DE HEER IOHANES WILMERDONX OVER DEKEN.

Reverse.—A binder's hand-press in which is a book; and a binder's plough. From the right side a man's hand issues holding a large flat hammer. The surrounding legend, reading on from the Obverse, is : PIETER VAN GOETHEN DEKEN.

HAARLEM. 1640?

Plate K.

Obverse.—A female figure representing Typography, her right hand holding a laurel wreath, and her left resting upon the bar-handle of a printing-press. Rays of light descend upon her head. Upon her right a stone pillar rises, emblematical of durability, upon which is engraved the word TYPOGRAHIA (*sic*). Over the pillar is the letter S, and over the press the letter C, for Senatus Consulto. In the Exergue is only the word HARLEMUM.

Reverse.—A ship in full sail, with a curiously notched beak at her prow, is breaking the heavy chains drawn across the entrance of a port (Damietta). On each side is a fortress where waves the Turkish flag, and whence the enemy is showering down arrows. Over all is the motto of the city of Haärlem, VICIT VIM VIRTUS, the arms of the city occupying the Exergue.

HAARLEM. 1640?

PLATE L.

Obverse.—A reduced facsimile of the last, with the word TYPOGRAPHIA, which is engraved upon the stone pillar, spelt correctly.

Reverse.—A reduced facsimile, in every particular, of the last.

LILLE. 1650?

PLATE M.

Obverse.—The figure of Typography, her right hand holding a pressman's inking ball, and her left supporting a sword, the point of which rests upon the ground.

Reverse.—Blank for the name of the Guild-member.

ABRAHAM ELSEVIER.

Leyden, 1652.

PLATE N.

[AN OVAL MEDAL.]

Obverse.—The goddess Minerva, with plumed head-dress and flowing robes, standing upon a platform. From her right hand depends a Medusa's head, and her left arm embraces a standard, upon which are the cross-keys, the arms of the city of Leyden. The legend upon the left side is ACAD-LVGD., and upon the right, BATAV.

Reverse.—An inscription only, in bold letters, consisting of eight short lines: ABRAHAMVS ELSEVIRIVS ACAD. LVGD. BATAV. TYPOGRAPHVS ANNO MƆCLII.

AMSTERDAM. 1659.

PLATE O.

Obverse.—A winged Mercury, with a caduceus in his right, and a book in his left hand, descends upon an open book. Upon the left is a binder's hand-press and a binder's plough; a pair of pressman's inking balls and a pair of compasses being on the right.

Reverse.—An ornamental, curved cartoon, left blank for the Guild-member's name, over which are the arms of the city of Amsterdam, with the civic crown as a crest, and two lions rampant as supporters.

HAARLEM. 1660?

Plate P.

Obverse.—A female seated figure, helmeted, representing Haarlem, rests her right foot upon a vase, whence flows water, and upon the rim of which is the name of the river running through Haarlem, SPARE. Her right hand holds a shield, upon which is the head of Medusa, and in her left hand is a laurel wreath and a model of the ship of Damietta. Behind her is a printing-press, upon which is an urn pouring forth types into a composing case beneath. To the left is a fortress attacked by the enemy, over which are the words ARTE ET MARTE. In the Exergue, DAM : CAPT : TYP : INV : URB DEFEN :

Reverse.—The figure of Prudence seated upon a bale of goods. The forefinger of her left hand is placed upon her lips, the elbow resting upon a volume

and Jettons. 13

bearing the letters S. C. (Senatus Consulto). The volume is placed upon a pedestal, upon which are the arms of Haarlem, and the motto VICIT VIM VIRTUS. In the lap of Prudence is an urn full of medals, one of which she is holding out with her right hand. The legend is : COMES CONSILIORUM. The Exergue bears the word HARLEM only.

HAARLEM. 1660?

Q (NO PLATE).

Obverse.—An imitation of the last.

Reverse.—An imitation of the last.

New dies were cut for this medal, variations appearing in both Obverse and Reverse ; but the best distinguishing mark will be seen in the Exergue of the Reverse, where the word HARLEM appears without the signs of contraction in the former medal, while in this there is a colon after it, thus, HARLEM :

GOTHA. 1700.

Plate R.

Obverse.—Aurora standing in a winged chariot is drawn by a winged horse in full speed upon the clouds. In her right hand she holds a lighted torch, and with her left scatters flowers upon the earth. Behind is the rising Sun, and upon the front of the chariot is a Cock, the herald of morn, while before her the brightness of the morning star grows dim. The legend, one half of which occupies the Exergue, is : VT AVRORA MVSIS AMICA SOLEM. ‖ SIC TYPOGRAPHIA RENATVM EVANGELIVM.

Reverse.—The inscription only :—ARTI TYPOGRAPHICÆ A IO : GVTTENBERGIO ARGENTORATI INVENTÆ AC OPE CONSILIOQ. IOAN. FAVSTI MOGVNTIÆ AN. MCCCCL. BIBLIIS LATINIS AENEO CHARACTERE IMPRESSIS PRIMVM VVLGATÆ QVINTVM JVBILAEVM ANNO CHRISTI IVBILAEO MDCC FELICITER CELEBRANTI SACRVM.

PARIS. 1723.

PLATE S.

Obverse.—Land and sea, typical of our world, above which is a mass of clouds. Upon these rests an open printed volume in the full rays of an unclouded Sun. Around is the legend: EX UTROQUE LUX ; and in the Exergue, in three short lines : BIBLIOPOLÆ ET TYPOGRAPHI PARIS.

Reverse.—The arms of the Booksellers and Printers of Paris, surmounted by a crown, and supported by two Sphinxes, couchant. In the Exergue is the date :
M.DCC.XXIII.

JOHN ANTONY VOLPI.

Verona, 1737.

PLATE T.

Obverse.—The bust of Volpi to the right, in the dress of a Professor, and wearing a flowing wig. The surrounding legend is : IO . ANTONIVS . VVLPIVS . ELOQV . PROF . IN GYMN PAT . CIƆIƆCCXXXVII.

Reverse.—The Arms of the city of Verona to the left, surrounded with ornaments. A victor's wreath of bay leaves, tied with a flowing ribbon, to the right. The surrounding legend is : * GAVDET VERONA CATVLLO * DE . CIVE SVO B M.

ALTDORF. 1740.

V (NO PLATE).

[The Author has been unable at present to discover any particulars of the above medal.]

ANSPACH. 1740.

X (NO PLATE).

[The Author has been unable at present to discover any particulars of the above medal.]

BASLE. 1740.

Plate Y.

Obverse.—Typography, personified by a woman with flowing robes and the winged head-dress of Mercury, is seated in a room at the back of which is a curtain and a window. To her right is an old wooden printing-press, against which leans a folio form of types; upon the press appears the date 1440. To her left is a compositor's case, and in front of her stands a short classic pillar. She holds in her right hand an inking-ball, and in her left a composing stick. In the Exergue: RERUM TUTISSIMA CUSTOS.

Reverse.—An inscription only, in bold letters:

ARTIS TYPOGR.
SACRIS SÆCULAR.
III
AVGVST. RAVRAC.
FELICITER CELEBR.
A. S. MDCCXL.

BRESLAU. 1740.
PLATE Z.

Obverse.—A three-quarter bust of Gutenberg on the left, opposite a three-quarter bust of Faust on the right. Behind the former the initials I. G. and behind the latter I. F. Over their heads the legend: DER BUCHDRUCKERKUNST, which is continued in the Exergue, ERFINDER 1440 ZV MAINZ.

Reverse.—The Printer's Arms, beneath which is the following inscription:

ALS GVTTENBERG VND FAVST
DER BVCHERDRVCK
ERDACHT
WARD
WARHEIT VND VERSTAND
IN HELLES LICHT
GEBRACHT

In the Exergue:

... DRITTES IVBILÆVM
1740
D. 24. IVN.

DRESDEN. 1740.

2 A (NO PLATE).

[The Author has been unable at present to discover any particulars of the above medal.]

ERFUHRT. 1740.

PLATE 2 B.

Obverse.—A bust upon a pedestal which bears the name GUTTEMBERG. Fame in her flight places a laurel crown upon the bust. On the flag of her trumpet are the Arms of Mayence. In the distance is a town with buildings and steeples, over which is the word MAINTZ. On either side of the pedestal are books

labelled CORP IU.—BIBLIA—ARISTOT.—
HIPPOC. Around the whole is the legend :
DIGNA VIRO PRO TALIBUS AUSIS.
In the Exergue :
IUBIL. III. TYPOGR :
CELEB. 1740.

Reverse.—Minerva taking by the hand Typographia, a figure whose dress is covered with letters, and whose head is surrounded with her name, TYPOGRAPHIA. Reclining upon the ground is Time, holding in his right hand the emblem of eternity, a serpent tail in mouth, which encloses three C's, to denote theft three centuries elapsed since the invention of printing. At the feet of Minerva is a Medusa's head, and behind her, an owl. The legend is : FELICI FŒDERE CRESCUNT ; and in the Exergue is the name of the engraver, WERNER FECIT.

GOTHA. 1740.

Plate 2 C.

Obverse.—From the same die as the Obverse of R.

Reverse.—The following inscription only:

ARTI.
TYPOGRAPHICAE.
A . IO . GVTENBERGIO .
ARGENTOR . INVENTAE .
OPE . CONSILIOQVE .
IO . FAVSTI . MOGVNTIAE .
AB . A . MCCCCXL . EXCVLTAE .
IVBILAEVM . TERTIVM .
ANNO . MDCCXL .
GOTHAE . IN . ANTIQVA .
REYHERORVM .
OFFICINA . FELICITER .
CELEBRANTI .
SACRVM .

✲

This is an adaptation of the Reverse of Medal R to suit the year 1740.

and Jettons. 23

GOTTINGEN. 1740.

PLATE 2 D.

Obverse.—The arms of the Guttenberg family resting upon a slab bearing the inscription : INSIGNIA . GENTILIT . EIVSDEM. In a very small Exergue is the letter K, being the initial of the engraver's name, Koch. Around all is the impious legend : DISSIMVLARE . HVNC . VIRVM . DISSIMVLARE . DEVM . EST.

Reverse.—Inscription only :

*

MEMOR . FEL .
IO . GVTTENBERG .
NOBIL . MOGVNT .
ANNO . SEC . III . CHALCOGR .
MDCCXXXX .
AEREO MONVM . MERITO
COLENDI
QVI . ARTE . A . SE . INVENTA
AERE . IMPRESSOS . LIBROS .
DEDIT . NOBIS .
AERE . MODICO .
PARARE

*

HAARLEM. 1740.

Plate 2 E.

[The Great Holtzhey.]

Obverse.—The city of Haarlem under the form of a Matron sitting upon a throne. In her left hand are the Roman fasces, from which hang three serpents, encircled one within another, denoting three centuries. With her right hand she makes an offering upon an altar, upon the front of which is represented the famous ship of Damiette. Over her head are the Arms of the city of Haarlem, together with those of the four Burgomasters in office during the festival. In the foreground are shown the chief products for which the city is celebrated, Yarn and Tulips. Two Cupids are employed in cultivating the latter, while a third is reading a book, upon which the title "SPIEGEL ONSER BEHOUDENISSE" appears. This is said to be the first book printed by Coster with moveable types.

and Jettons. 25

Across the river at the back are seen the churches and buildings of Haarlem. The legend is MEMORIAE SACRVM. In the Exergue is HARLEMVM. MDCCXL. ; and upon the border, M. HOLTZHEY FECIT.

Reverse.—The wood near Haarlem, where Coster is seated upon the stump of a tree, his name appearing in small letters upon the hem of his tunic. In his right hand is the letter A, which he has just cut upon a piece of wood. His left is extended, and he seems to speak with Wisdom, which under the form of Minerva descends upon him from the clouds. The rays from heaven which fall upon him over the head of Minerva shew that the art of Printing originated from a still higher source, coming direct from heaven itself. To the left is a miniature printing-press and materials, with which three Cupids are busily working. Exergue : TYPOGRAPHIA HIC PRIMVM INVENTA CIRCA ANN. MCCCCXL. Upon the border are the initials of the engraver, M. H.

HAARLEM. 1740.

Plate 2 F.

[The Small Holtzhey.]

Obverse.—A three-quarter bust of Coster to the right, the left hand holding up to view the letter A. Legend: LAVRENTIVS COSTERVS HARLEMENSIS PRIMVS ARTIS TYPOGRAPHICAE INV. CIRCA A. MCCCCXL. Beneath the right arm is the engraver's name: M. HOLTZHEY. F.

Reverse.—Inscription:

DE DRUKKUNST NU DRIE EEUWEN OUDT
   DOOR KOSTER VOORTGETEELD
UIT BEUKESCHORS, IN 'T HAERLEMSCH HOUT
   AENSCHOUDT HAER'S VADERS BEELDT
OP DIT METAEL, EN ROEPT VERBLYDT,
   DIT MANNELYK GELAET,
ZY AEN DE ONSTERFLYKHEIT GEWYDT
   ZOOLANG DE WERELD STAET.

Above this inscription is a garland of

laurel, across which salterwise are the trumpet of Fame and the torch of Truth. Within the garland is an open book, upon which appears in very small letters SPIEGEL ONS. BEHOUDEN, being the name of the first book in moveable types attributed to the press of Coster. Beneath the inscription are three serpents intertwined, with a branch of palm and a branch of bay, and in the centre the Arms of the city of Haarlem, beneath which are the engraver's initials, M. H.

HAARLEM. 1740.

PLATE 2 G.

[THE GREAT MARSHOORN.]

Obverse.—The bust of Coster in profile to the left, with the legend : LAUR . JANSZ . KOSTER . HARL. Beneath are the initials of the engraver, G. M. F.

Reverse.—A printing-press against one end of which rests a shield bearing the Arms of the city of Haarlem: at the other end is an open book "SPIEGEL ONSER BEHOUDENISE 1440," the earliest book printed by Coster. To the left in bold letters, TYP. INV. 1428. Near the press is a shield bearing a dove, the device of Coster. At foot in a cartoon is the engraver's name, G. MARSHOORN, and in the Exergue is the date 1740. The whole is surrounded by three serpents forming a circle, each holding the tail of another in its mouth.

HAARLEM. 1740.

PLATE 2 H.

[THE LITTLE MARSHOORN.]

Obverse.—Bust of Coster with profile to the left, wearing a cap and senatorial collar of fur. Legend: LAUR. COSTERUS

JANI F. SEN. HARL. TYP. INV. Beneath the bust in small characters the name of the engraver, G. MARSHOORN HARL. FEC.

Reverse.—A printing-press, on the head of which is a shield bearing the Arms of the city of Haarlem, and upon the "winter" or cross piece, through which the screw works, a shield bearing a dove, the device of Coster. Against the press leans an open volume, upon which appears :

SPE   SAL
CUL-   VATI
HUMA ONIS

(Speculum humani salvationis) the title of one of the earliest books attributed by Dutch bibliographers to the press of Coster. The legend is : INV. 1428. PERVULG. 1440. III JUB. 1740. In the Exergue :

TYPOGRAPHIA
HARLEMI
G. M.

HAARLEM. 1740.

Plate 2 I.

[The Great Van Swindern.]

Obverse.—The bust of Coster to the left, with cap on his head, and official fur collar over his shoulders, placed upon a pedestal bearing the words ALTER CADMUS. Behind the bust is a printing-press, and to the right is a wreath of laurel and a pot of flowers, upon which is the letter H. In front is a serpent, tail in mouth, placed against a pile of books, upon which burns an antique lamp. By the side of the lamp is an open volume bearing the words:

SP :   ONS
BEH :   NIS
1440

The legend is : ✱ LAUR. I. COSTERUS. CONS. HARLEM. TYPOGR. INVENT. AD' AN : MDCCCCXL.

Reverse.—The Arms of the city of Haarlem supported by two lions, and resting upon the Roman fasces and palm and laurel boughs. The city appears in the back-ground, over which a winged figure is flying bearing the first printed book in her right, and a trumpet in her left hand, upon the flag of which appears the word FAMA. The legend is: HINC TOTUM SPARGUNTUR IN ORBEM LITERÆ; and under the feet of the right-hand lion the initials N. V. S. F. In the Exergue: PER TRIA SECULA · MDCCXL.

HAARLEM. 1740.

PLATE 2 K.

[THE LITTLE VAN SWINDERN.]

Obverse.—The bust of Coster to the left, around which is the legend: L. I. COSTERUS. CONS. HARL. TYP. INV. AD. AN. 1440.

Reverse.—Typography personified by a female figure in flowing robes, upon whose head divine rays descend. In her right hand, suspended from a garland of laurel leaves, are seven ovals bearing the Arms of the officials of Haarlem at the period of the Jubilee. Her left arm supports a shield bearing the Arms of the city of Haarlem half-hidden behind her figure, and from her hand escapes a scroll upon which are the vowels A. E. I. O. U. She treads under foot a book upon which are the letters A. G. for " Alexandri Grammatica," said to be the first book printed by Gutenberg at Mayence, with the types which he stole from his master, Coster. The legend is : EX HIS TIBI NECTE CORONAM. To the right N. V. S. F., being the initials of the engraver, and in the Exergue the words :

TYPOGR. HAERLEM.
III IUBIL. 1740.

LEIPSIG. 1740.

PLATE 2 L.

Obverse.—Typographia between a printing-press and a compositor's case, holding in one hand a composing-stick, and in the other a pair of inking-balls. The legend is : SPES . O . FIDISSIMA . MVSIS.
In the Exergue :
ANNO TYPOGRAPHIAE
SECVLARI TERTIO
MDCCXL.

Reverse.—A Muse, holding in her right hand a manuscript, to whom a winged Genius is shewing a printed book. The legend is :
NOVAS . MIRABITVR . ARTES.
In the Exergue :
FELIX . INVENTVM .
GERMANIAE .
MCCCCXL.

LEIPSIG. 1740.

Plate 2 M.

Obverse.—Gutenberg and Fust face to face. Legend: IOH . GVTTENBERG . IOH . FAVSTVS.
In the Exergue:

>TYPOGRAPHIAE
>INVENTORES
>MAGONTIACI
>MCCCCXL.

Reverse.—A printing-press, near to which, seated on a bale of paper, is a female figure holding in her right hand a pair of inking-balls. A composing-stick is in her left hand, which rests upon a shield bearing the Printer's Arms. The legend is: ARS VICTVRA DVM LITTERIS MANEBIT PRETIVM.

In the Exergue:

ANNO TYP. SAECVL. III.
GRATA POSTERITAS
EXCVDIT . MDCCXL.

beneath which in small letters :

I. DASSIER. F.

This medal is commonly but erroneously attributed to Geneva because Dassier resided there. It was, however, a commission from the Leipsig University, and was distributed in that city upon the occasion of the Typographical Jubilee.

NUREMBERG. 1740.

Plate 2 N.

Obverse.—The figure of Germany with the Imperial crown on her head, sitting on a throne, her right hand holding the sceptre, and her left a horn of plenty. At her feet are the globe and a sword, emblems of power and justice. Wisdom, around whose head rays of divine light

play, is placing a laurel wreath upon the head of Germany, an olive branch being in her left hand. Between the two figures is the Roman eagle. To the left is a printing-press, and surrounding the whole is the legend, AVSPICIO IMPERII SVMMAE DECVS ADDITVR ARTIS. In the Exergue, FELIX GERMANIA, beneath which is v. for Vestner the engraver.

Reverse.—An altar, upon which is placed an open volume bearing the words:

BIB   SA

LIA   CRA

books of all sizes covering the ground. The surrounding legend is:

TVIS HIC OMNIA PLENA MVNERIBVS.

The name JAH in Hebrew letters, in an illuminated triangle, throws its radiance upon the book.

In the Exergue is:

MEMORIA IVBIL. III.

TYPOGRAPHIAE

MDCCXL.

NUREMBERG. 1740.

PLATE 2 O.

Obverse.—A printing-press with a Genius on either side, one holding a composing-stick, and the other the inking-balls used by pressmen. Over the press flies Fame blowing a trumpet, and bearing in her left hand a scroll, upon which are emblazoned the names of GUTTENBERG, FAUST, SCHEFFER, MENTELIN, REGIOMONT. The surrounding legend is: BENEFICIO DEI ET SOLERTIA GERMANORVM. In the Exergue:
MEMOR . SAECVLAR .
CIƆIƆCCXXXX.

Reverse.—A garland of laurel, in which five coats of armour are interwoven. The uppermost is the shield of Nuremberg, the other four belonging to the Four Curators "rei sacrae et literariae." In the centre is the following inscription:

DEO OPT . MAX .
OB BENEFICIVM
TYPOGRAPH . A GERM .
INVENTAE ET PER III SAEC
FELICITER EXCVLTAE
VOTA SOLV . ET MVLTIPL.
TYPOGRAPHI NORIMB.

In the Exergue:

CVRAT . REI SACR.
ET LITER.

NUREMBERG. 1740.

PLATE 2 F.

Obverse.—Eternity, personified by an aged man with a serpent, tail in mouth, encircling him, descends from the clouds and offers to Germany, who appears in the form of Minerva, a scroll bearing the letters A B C. Upon her breast are the

national arm, and surrounding her are boys representing the four quarters of the globe, as symbolised by the ornaments on their heads, each being busy with various implements of the art. One has a typefounder's mould, another is "working at case," another has a pair of inking-balls, and the fourth exhibits a printed sheet. The surrounding legend is : GLORIA GERMANORVM LVCRVM ORBIS. Beneath, in small letters, are I. L. Œ. the initials of the engraver, Johann Laurent Oechsel, and quite at foot the letter N for Nürnberger the Master of the Mint.

Reverse.—An inscription surrounded with a laurel wreath :

D. G.
IVBILÆVM TERTIVM
ÆTERNÆ ARTIS
TYPOGRAPHICÆ
MDCCXXXX.

NUREMBERG. 1740.

Plate 2 Q.

[The Eight Printers.]

Obverse.—The Arms of the city of Nuremberg surrounded by a garland of palm and laurel branches, in which are four coats of arms, over each of which the initials of one of the four Curators is engraved.   Without any inscription.

Reverse.—A central inscription :

ZVM
ANDENKEN
DES III IVBEL-FESTES
SO· DIE VIII. DRVCKEREYEN
IN NVRNBERG
GEFEYRET HABEN.

1740.

Surrounding the whole are eight cartoons interwoven with ribbon, each cartoon bearing the monogram of a printer of Nuremberg.

RATISBON. 1740.

PLATE 2 R.

Obverse.—The Arms of the city of Ratisbon sustained in the claws of the Imperial eagle, and illumined by the eye of divine Providence. To the left is a composing-case, and to the right a printing-press, at each of which a Genius is working. The legend is: DECUS URBIS ET ARTIS. In the Exergue: MDCCXL.

Reverse.—An inscription only, within a wreath of laurel:

SACRA
DEI HONORI
AVG CAROLI VI IMPERIO
RATISPONÆ GLORIÆ
ARTIS TYPOGRAPHICÆ
SÆC. III IUBIL.
CELEBRANTIS
MEMORIA.

In a trefoil below are the letters L L S.

BATH. 1794.

2 S (NO PLATE).

Obverse.—The Arms of the city of Bath, with supporters and crest, beneath which is the date 1794. In this the "bar wavy," soon after added, is omitted by mistake. The legend is:

W. GYE, PRINTER & STATIONER, BATH.

Reverse.—The figure of Benevolence sitting upon a bale of goods. At her feet are bags of money. Her left hand holds an olive branch, the elbow resting upon a jar; with her right she is pointing to a prison, towards which a boy is going bearing a key, and with a scarf *flowing over his shoulder.* The words GO FORTH issue from rays of light. The legend is: REMEMBER THE DEBTORS OF ILCHESTER GOAL.

Rim.—PAYABLE AT W. TEBAYS, HASTINGS. Examples with the proper rim, as in the following number, are very rare.

BATH. 1794.

PLATE 2 T.

Obverse.—The same as the last, with the "bar wavy" added to the die.

Reverse.—A copy of the last, with the variation of the boy's scarf *flowing across his hips.*

Rim.—PAYABLE AT W. GYE'S, PRINTER, BATH.

There is another variation, in which the Obverse is from the same die as above, the Reverse being from a new die. It may be distinguished by the boy's scarf *flowing over both shoulder and hips.*

LONDON. 1794.

Plate 2 U.

Obverse.—A very imperfect representation of a printing-press, beneath which is the date 1794. The legend is: SIC ORITUR DOCTRINA SURGETQUE LIBERTAS.

Reverse.—Inscription only:

PAYABLE
AT
THE FRANKLIN PRESS
LONDON.

LONDON. 1795.

Plate 2 X.

Obverse.—Bust of Eaton to the left, with a ribbon underneath, upon which, in small letters, is the motto:
FRANGAS NON FLECTES.
The surrounding legend is:
D. I. EATON THREE TIMES ACQUITTED OF SEDITION.

Reverse.—A pig-stye with four pigs, one of which is holding up a book in his mouth. Upon a part of the rails stands a dunghill Cock in full plumage.
The legend is:
PRINTER TO THE MAJESTY OF THE PEOPLE LONDON . 1795.

LAMBETH. 1796.

Plate 2 Y.

Obverse.—Inscription only, in very rude characters:

> Denton.
> Engraver
> &. Printer
> 7. Mead Row.
> . near. the.
> Asylum.
> Lambeth.

Reverse.—A wheat-sheaf, in which is a sickle, between two starlings, with the figures 17 on the left, and 96 on the right. A border of separate oak leaves surrounds the whole.

LAMBETH. 1796?

PLATE 2 Z.

Obverse.—Struck from the same die as the preceding.

Reverse.—Within a border of single laurel leaves are the two towers of the gateway of Lambeth Palace, with tall trees behind, and a rail to the left.

LAMBETH. 1798?

PLATE 3 A.

Obverse.—The same as Plate 2 Y.

Reverse.—A very meagre wreath of oak leaves, within which are the Prince of Wales's feathers and a ribbon with the motto ICH DIEN.

J. B. BODONI.

Parma, 1802.

PLATE 3 B.

Obverse.—The bust of Bodoni to the left, under which in minute letters: L. MANFREDINI F. The legend is: IOHANNES. BAPTISTA. BODONIVS. MDCCCII.

Reverse.—Within a laurel wreath this inscription:
> CIVI . OPTIMO .
> DECVRIONI . SOLERTISS .
> ARTIS . TYPOGRAPHICAE .
> CORYPHAEO . ERVDITISS .
> EX . XII . VIRVM . PARM .
> DECRETO.

GRASS AND BARTH.

Breslau, 1804.

PLATE 3 C.

Obverse.—A sleeping lion, against whose body leans a shield bearing the device or Arms of Baumgarten, the first Breslau printer. Above is the imperial Eagle encircled with rays of light, whilst two other attributes of the press are symbolised by the sceptre and the Caduceus. In the Exergue is the date 1504.

Reverse.—Inscription only, with a small branch beneath the foot-line :

DREI-
HUNDERTIÆHRIGES
IUBILÆUM
DER
GRASS UND BARTHSCHEN
STADTBUCHDRUCKEREY
ZU BRESLAU
1804.

IMPERIAL PRINTING OFFICE.

Paris, 1809.

PLATE 3 D.

Obverse.—The bust of the Emperor Napoleon I. to the right, beneath which, in small letters, ANDRIEU F., and around which is the legend:

NAPOLEON EMP. ET ROI.

Reverse.—Within a wreath of oak and myrtle leaves this inscription:

JMPRIMERIE
JMPÉRIALE.
DÉCRET DU XXIV. MARS
M.DCCC.IX.

Space is left beneath for the insertion of a number.

PARIS. 1818.

PLATE 3 E.

Obverse.—Bust of Gutenberg to the right, with a fur cap upon his head, and a long beard. Legend:

JOANNES GUTTEMBERG.

Beneath the bust in small letters,

GAYRARD F.

Reverse.—Inscription only:

NATUS
MOGUNTIÆ
IN GERMANIA
AN. M. CCCC.
OBIIT
AN. M.CCCC.LXVIII.

SERIES NUMISMATICA
UNIVERSALIS VIRORUM ILLUSTRIUM.

M.DCCC.XVIII.
DURAND EDIDIT.

PARIS. 1818.

Plate 3 F.

Obverse.—A similar bust to the last, but without the cap. Legend, the same.

Reverse.—A copy of the last. This medal is the same size as the next, and a little smaller than 3 E.

PARIS. 1818.

3 G (no plate).

Obverse.—The same as last. This variety is distinguished by having the letter H in JOHANNES, the two previous medals having it JOANNES.

Reverse.—The same as last.

PARIS. 1820.

PLATE 3 H.

Obverse.—Victory, in a chariot drawn by four horses, is galloping over Europe casting the conqueror's wreaths upon the various countries.

Reverse.—Within a wreath composed of laurel and oak leaves tied together with a ribbon, is the following inscription :

LES
SOUSCRIPTEURS
ASSOCIÉS
POUR TRANSMETTRE
A LA POSTÉRITÉ
LES VICTOIRES ET CONQUÊTES
DES FRANCAIS
DE 1792 A 1815.
ÉDITEUR
C. L. F. PANCKOUCKE
1820.

PIERRE DIDOT.

Paris, 1823.

Plate 3 I.

Obverse.—A bust to the right, around which is: PIERRE DIDOT L'AINE TYPOGRAPHE FRANCAIS, and in small characters beneath, VEYRAT F.

Reverse.—An iron printing-press, against the T of which is: PRESSE JULES DIDOT. On the left side of the press is the "ball-rack," in which is a pair of pressman's inking-balls. The surrounding legend is: HORACE, VIRGILE, RACINE, LAFONTAINE ED^{ons} IN-FOL^o; and in small letters, VEYRAT F. 1823.

HAARLEM. 1823.

Plate 3 K.

Obverse.—Science, represented by an Angel with a robe over her right arm, the hand supporting a lighted torch, whose beams are scattered around. The left hand rests upon a shield bearing the Arms of North Holland, behind which is a pile of books printed by Coster, surmounted by a palm branch. To the left is a printing-press, upon the platten of which is the word SPIEGHEL. At the head of the press is Coster's device, a Dove bearing an olive branch. Upon the ground is an open volume bearing the words DONATUS GRAM. QUID. The Arms of the city of Haarlem upon a shield rest against the volume, and surrounding the whole is the legend: LAUS URBI LUX ORBI. In the Exergue: CIƆCCCCXX — CIƆCCCCXXV. BRAEMT FECIT.

Reverse.—An inscription, surrounded by a wreath of oak-leaves:

> SAECULARE IV
> TYPOGRAPHIAE
> INVENTAE
> HARLEMI
> A
> LAUR. JANI F. COSTERO.

Outside the wreath is: CELEBRATUM HARLEMI X JULII CIƆIƆCCCXXIII.

HAARLEM. 1823.

Plate 3 L.

Obverse.—The monument erected in 1823 in the wood near Haarlem, with a grove of trees behind. In the Exergue the Arms of the city of Haarlem, and on the border the initials of the engravers' names, D. V. & Z.

and Jettons.

Reverse.—An inscription surrounded with a laurel wreath, broken at top by a cartouche, in which is the letter A, with wings; a symbol which is also engraved upon the front of the monument. On the left it is broken by a circle surrounding a square, within which is the symbol of eternity, a serpent, tail in mouth; and on the right by a similar figure containing a lamp burning. The inscription is as follows:

<pre>
         TER EERE VAN
        LOURENS JANSZ.
            KOSTER.
           UITVINDER
              DER
         BOEKDRUKKUNST
             DOOR
         BURGEMEESTEREN
       EN RADEN DER STAD
            HAARLEM.
      OP HET IV EEUWGETYDE
           MDCCCXXIII.
</pre>

HAARLEM. 1823.

3 M (NO PLATE).

Obverse.—The same as the last.
Reverse.—A new die, with slight but very evident variations.

HAARLEM. 1823.

PLATE 3 N.

Obverse.—A cast from the Obverse of Plate 2 F.
Reverse.—A cast (probably from an engraved wood-block) of the following inscription:

VIERDE
EEUW-FEEST
der
BOEKDRUKKUNST
Gevierd binnen
HAARLEM,
10 en 11 julij
1823.

ROYAL PRINTING OFFICE.

Paris, 1823.

PLATE 3 O.

Obverse.—A bust in profile to the left, around which is this legend : LVDOVICVS. XVIII. REX. FRANC. ET. NAV., and in very small characters the engraver's name, DEPAULIS F. In the Exergue :

TYPOGRAPHIA REGIA
RESTITVTA
MDCCCXXIII.

Reverse.—Inscription only :

A
FRANCISCO I
CONDITA MDXXXIX
LVDOVICO XIII
IN ÆDIBVS REGIIS
COLLOCATA MDCXL
LVDOVICO MAGNO
ILLVSTRATA
MDCXC.

ROYAL PRINTING OFFICE.

Paris, 1831.

PLATE 3 P.

Obverse.—Laureated bust to the left, with the surrounding legend: LVDOV. PHILIPPVS . I FRANCORVM . REX. In the Exergue:

TYPOGRAPHIA REGIA
INSTAVRATA
MDCCCXXXI.

Beneath the bust, in very small letters, DEPAULIS F.

Reverse.—Inscription only:

A
FRANCISCO I
CONDITAM MDXXXIX
LVDOVICVS XIII
IN ÆD. REG. COLLOCAVIT
LVDOVICVS XIV
SVMPT. REG. INSTRVXIT.
TANDEM. NAPOLEO
NOV. INCREM. AVCTAM
PVBL. ET LITT. VTILIT.
DESTINAVIT.
MDCCCIX.

PARIS. 1836?

Plate 3 Q.

[AN OCTAGON JETTON.]

Obverse.—The busts of Gutenberg and Senefelder in profile to the right. On the left side,
>GUTTEMBERG. 1436

and on the right,
>SENEFELDER. 1796

Reverse.—A wreath of oak and laurel, inside of which is the monogram *P D*, and outside of which to the left,
>IMPRIMERIE

above,
>LIBRAIRIE

to the right,
>LITHOGRAPHIE

and below,
>PAUL DUPONT ET CIE.

AUGSBURG. 1837.

Plate 3 R.

Obverse.—The Thorwaldsen statue of Gutenberg, around which is the legend: MON. IO. GVTENBERGII P. M. D. XIV AVG. MDCCCXXXVII. MOGVNT. INAVGVR. Beneath the pedestal is the engraver's name, NEUSS F.

Reverse.—An inscription only:

ARTEM
QUAE GRAECOS LATVIT
LATVITQVE LATINOS,
GERMANI SOLERS
EXTVDIT INGENIVM.
NUNC QVIDQVID
VETERES SAPIVNT,
SAPIVNTQVE RECENTES
NON SIBI,
SED POPVLIS OMNIBVS
ID SAPIVNT.

BERLIN. 1837.

PLATE 3 S.

Obverse.—The Thorwaldsen statue of Gutenberg erected in Mayence in 1837. The legend is: IOANNI GENSFLEISCH DICT. GVTENBERG COLLATIONIBVS TOTIVS EVROPAE SIGN. POS. In the Exergue:
THORWALDSEN
INV. ET DIR.

Reverse.—Gutenberg seated at a table explains the newly-discovered art to the astonished Schöffer. The legend is: INVENTORI ARTIS TYPOGRAPH. IN URBE PATRIA PIA LAETANTE. In the Exergue:
MOGONTIACI M. AVGVST.
MDCCCXXXVII.
EX OFF. MON. G. LOOS.
Beneath the feet of Schœffer in small letters: H. LORENZ F. ROMAE.

BERLIN. 1837.

PLATE 3 T.

Obverse.—The bust of Gutenberg copied from the Thorwaldsen statue, with the legend: GUTENBERG ERFINDER D. BUCHDRUCKERKUNST.

Reverse.—The full-length statue from the Thorwaldsen monument, with the legend: ERRICHTET ZU MAINZ AM 14 AUGUST 1837.

MAYENCE. 1837.

3 U.

[See PLATE Z.]

Obverse.—The Thorwaldsen statue of Gutenberg, around which is the legend:
IN MEMORIAM XIV AVG. MDCCCXXXVII.

Reverse.—Inscription only:

*
IOHANNEM GENSFLEISCH
DE GUTENBERG.
PATRICIUM MOGUNTINUM.
AERE PER TOTAM EUROPAM COLLATO
POSUERUNT CIVES.
MDCCCXXXVII.

PARIS. 1837.

Plate 3 X.

Obverse.—A rude press, with a pair of inking-balls on the right, and a type-founder's mould upon the left. The legend is:

LUMEN AD REVELATIONEM GENTIUM.

In the Exergue:
ANNO D.
MCCCCL.

and in very minute characters:
GIRAUD F.

Reverse.—A wreath of oak-leaves and acorns, outside of which is: FONDERIE GÉNÉRALE DES CARACTÉRES FRANÇAIS ET ETRANGERS, 1837.; and inside:
COMITÉ
CONSULTATIF
D'ART
TYPOGRAPHIQUE.

PARIS. 1837.

Plate 3 Y.

[AN OCTAGON-SHAPED MEDAL.]

Obverse.—Within a bold wreath of myrtle leaves, tied at foot with a ribbon :
IMPRIMERIE
LANGE LÉVY
ET COMP^{IE}.

1ER. AOUT 1837.

Reverse.—Within a similar wreath, of which the half to the right is oak-leaves, and the left, myrtle :
MEMBRES
DU
CONSEIL

TURIN. 1837.

Plate 3 Z.

Obverse.—Bust to the right, with the name on either side,

CAROLO BOVCHERONO

the remainder of the sentence being upon the Reverse.

Reverse.—An inscription within a wreath of laurel, continued from the Obverse :

OB
EGREGIAM OPERAM
IN EDITIONEM
SCRIPTORVM LATINOR.
COLLATAM
J. POMBA TYP.
M. DCCC. XXX. VII.

FIRMIN DIDOT.

Paris, 1839.

PLATE 4 A.

Obverse.—A bust, nearly full face, to the right, in modern costume, with the name, on either side, in bold letters:
FIRMIN DIDOT.

Reverse.—A heavy wreath of laurel leaves, tied at foot with a ribbon, within which is this inscription:
STEPHANORUM
ÆMULUS
MUSARUM
CULTOR

AUGSBURG. 1840.

Plate 4 B.

Obverse.—The Thorwaldsen statue of Gutenberg, around which is this irreverent legend, which is borrowed from the Dutch : DISSIMVLARE . VIRVM . HVNC . DISSIMVLARE . DEVM . EST.

Reverse.—A circular shield, in the centre of which is a Medusa's head surrounded by rays, and on the circumference 16 stars. The shield is supported on two oak branches, and is surmounted by a sphinx-crested helmet. The legend is : ARTE . SVA . LITERAS . AVXIT . — IN . MEMOR . SECVLAR. TYPOGRAPHIAE. MDCCCXL. Beneath the shield, in very minute characters, is

I. I. NEVSS F.

BAMBERG. 1840.

Plate 4 C.

Obverse.—A printing-press, upon which appears the date 1455, being the year in which the art was first practised in Bamberg. Upon a stool are a pair of inking-balls, and against the press a shield leans bearing the device of Albert Pfister, the first printer at Bamberg. Around is the legend : DEM ANDENKEN ALB. PFISTERS U. SEINER ERSTEN NACHFOLGER : J. U. L. SENSENSCHMIDT, H. PETZENSTEINER, J. PFEIL, H. SPORER, J. PERNECKER, U. M. AYRER. In the Exergue, in very small letters, is :

I. I. NEUSS F.

Reverse.—The city of Bamberg, over which is this legend : DAS KÖNIGL. BIBLIOTHEKAR. F. D. IV JUBELFEST D. BUCHDRUCKERKUNST 24 JUNI 1840 ZU BAMBERG. the last word being placed in the Exergue.

BAMBERG. 1840.

4 D (NO PLATE).

Obverse.—The same as Plate 4 G.

Reverse.—The same as Plate 4 G, with the exception of the Exergue, which, being adapted to this city, reads :

VIERTE IUBELF. D. ERFINDUNG
D. BUCHDRUCKERKUNST
IN DEUTSCHL
BAMBERG 24 IUNI 1840.

BASLE. 1840.

PLATE 4 E.

Obverse.—The bust of Froben to the right, around which is:
JOHANNES FROBENIUS.
Across the field, in small characters, is the engraver's name:
A. BOVY   FECIT.

Reverse.—An inscription only, occupying eight lines:
GEB. ZU
HAMELBURG. 1460.
GEST. ZU BASEL. 1527.

SAECULAR-FEIER
DER
BUCHDRUCKER-KUNST
IN BASEL
1840.

BERLIN. 1840.

Plate 4 F.

Obverse.—The bust of Gutenberg to the left, around which is the legend:

IOHANN GAENSFLEISCH gen. GUTENBERG

and beneath the bust:

GEB. Z. MAINZ ZWISCHEN 1393—1400.

Under the shoulder is:

LOOS D. KÖNIG F.

Reverse.—Gutenberg in his printing-office, which is represented as a grand vaulted chamber, with rich columns suitable to the position of a nobleman of Mayence. The famous printer is seated upon a stool reading a proof sheet. Before him is an antique press, and behind him a composing-case. Upon the wall is a map of Europe, rays of light issuing from Germany. Through the door is

and Jettons.

seen the sky, with the retiring stars of night. The legend is: DAS IST VOM HERRN GESCHEHEN UND EIN WUNDER VOR UNSEREN AUGEN * PS. 118 V. 23. In the Exergue :

> VIERTE IUBELF. D. ERFINDUNG
> D. BUCHDRUCKERKUNST
> IN DEUTSCHLAND
> D. 24 IUNI 1840

BERLIN. 1840.

PLATE 4 G.

Obverse.—A reduced facsimile of the last.

Reverse.—A reduced facsimile of the last, with the omission of the surrounding legend, and the addition of PS. 118. V. 23. upon the boundary line of the Exergue.

BERLIN. 1840.

Plate 4 H.

Obverse.—A three-quarter bust of Gutenberg to the right, with a small shield bearing Gutenberg's Arms to the left. Around in gothic letters is:

Johannes Gutenberg.

Upon the under edge of the bust is the engraver's name:

KRUGER F.

Reverse.—The Printer's Arms, surrounded by a ribbon, upon which, in sunk letters, appear the words

Der Welt die Warheit.

Around the whole is the legend:

**Vierte saecularfeier der Buchdruckerkunst
* Mdcccxxxx ***

COLOGNE. 1840.

PLATE 4 I.

Obverse.—The bust of Gutenberg to the left, with the legend surrounding it in a border: * JOHANN GAENSFLEISCH GENANNT GUTTENBERG GEBOREN ZU MAINZ UM 1393—1400 + 1465.

Reverse.—The Arms of Mayence, Cologne, and Strasbourg united together by a flowing ribbon, upon which are the words UND ES WARD LICHT. Rays of light dart from the centre to the circumference, where are the names:
AUGSBURG. FRANKFURT. NUERNBERG.
The legend surrounding the whole is:
ZUM ANDENKEN DER IV SAECULAR FEYER DER ERFINDUNG DER BUCHDRUCKERKUNST
* 1840 *

FRANKFORT. 1840.

Plate 4 K.

Obverse.—A representation of the stone monument erected in 1840 at Frankfort, upon the occasion of the Typographical Jubilee. The legend is:

GUTENBERG. FUST. SCHÖFFER.

Reverse.—A wreath of oak and laurel leaves, outside of which is: ZU EHREN DER ERFINDUNG DER BUCHDRUCKERKUNST * FRANKFURT $^A/_M$; and inside, in five lines:

BEI DER
4. SÄCULAR
FEIER
AM 24 JUNI
1840.

LEIPSIG. 1840.

Plate 4 L.

Obverse.—The Thorwaldsen Statue, with the word
GUTENBERG
in the Exergue.

Reverse.—The building erected at Leipsig for the Typographical Festival. In the Exergue, which occupies nearly one-half of the field:

FESTSALON Z : VIERT :
JUBILAEUM D : ERFIND :
D : BUCHDRUCKERK :
I : LEIPZIG
D. 24 . 25 . 26 . JUNI 1840.

LEIPSIG. 1840.

Plate 4 M.

Obverse.—The bust of Gutenberg to the right, with fur cap and fur cloak, around which is

IOHANNES GUTENBERG

Reverse.—A rude representation of the buildings used for the Typographical Jubilee at Leipsig in 1840. In the Exergue, which occupies nearly one-half of the field:

FESTSALON
Z . 4 . SAECULARFEIER
D. BUCHDRUCKERK
I. LEIPZIG
1840.

LEIPSIG. 1840.

PLATE 4 N.

Obverse.—A three-quarter bust of Gutenberg to the left, over which is the legend :

✻ IV . SAEC . F . D . BUCHDR . K . IN LEIPZIG
IOHANNES GUTENBERG

Beneath the bust, in small letters :

SCHRECK ed. WARTIG S.

Reverse.—A printing-press placed upon a large volume, the volume resting upon the Cross, and the whole supported by a sunlit cloud. Above is :

JESAIAS CAP. 9. V. 2.

Beneath is the city of Mayence, and in the Exergue the word :

MAINZ.

LEIPSIG. 1840.

4 O (NO PLATE).

Obverse.—The same as Plate 4 G.

Reverse.—The same as Plate 4 G, with the exception of the Exergue, which reads thus :

> VIERTE IUBELF. D. ERFINDUNG
> D. BUCHDRUCKERKUNST
> IN DEUTSCHL.
> LEIPZIG D. 24 IUNI 1840.

LEIPSIG. 1840.

PLATE 4 P.

Obverse.—The bust of Gutenberg to the right, around which is : ✱ JOHANNES GUTENBERG ✱ GEB : Z. MAINZ ZW : 1393— 1400. GEST : 1468.
Beneath the shoulder is the engraver's name,

EHRHARDT F.

Reverse.—A bust upon a pedestal, whereon, in very small letters, appears the word GUTTENBERG. Divine rays descend from above, while a Matron, personifying the city of Mayence, places a laurel wreath upon the bust, holding in her left hand a copy of the first printed bible. Beside her, upon the ground, are two more books, and close by, a square block bearing upon the front the Arms of Mayence encircled by laurel, and upon

its top a bee-hive in full activity. To the left are placed a printing-press and a composing-case. From the former drops a cornucopia, whence numerous books issue. Leaning against the base of the pedestal is an oval cartouche, upon which are seen two profiles and the words :

FAUST SCHÖFFER

in very small letters. In the Exergue :

VIERTE
SÄCULARFEIER

which is continued in the lower part of the circumference :

DER BUCHDRUCKERKUNST . 1840.

Over the whole is the legend :

* ZUM RUHME DES DEUTSCHEN VATERLANDES *

Beneath the woman's feet are the letters

E. F.

LYONS. 1840.

PLATE 4 Q.

Obverse.—Science, represented by a female figure in loose robes, surrounded by the emblems of Geometry, Geography, Painting, and Medicine, stands in front of a printing-press. In the background are rows of shelves full of books. The legend is :

SERVANDIS ARTIBUS UNA.

In the Exergue :

BIBLIOPOLÆ ET TYPOGRAPHI LUGDUN.

Reverse.—Two sphinxes, between whom is a pedestal supporting two oval shields, one bearing the Arms of the Printers and Booksellers of Paris, and the other the Arms of the city of Lyons.

LYONS. 1840.

Plate 4 R.

Obverse.—The profile busts of Gutenberg and Senefelder to the right. Legend :

  I. GUTENBERG. A. SENEFELDER.

Beneath the busts, in small characters, is the name of the engraver :

  PENIN F. LVGD.

Reverse.—An inscription only :

  SOCIÉTÉ
  DES IMPRIMEURS
  DE LYON.
  ———
  MDCCCXXXX
  IIII ANNIV. SECUL.
  DE L'INV. DE L'IMPR.

MAYENCE. 1840.

PLATE 4 S.

Obverse.—Three busts in profile to the right, over which are the names:
GUTENBERG.   FUST.   SCHOEFFER.

The legend is:
SIE GABEN MACHT DEM LICHT
DASS ES DIE NACHT DURCHBRICHT

Reverse.—The Printers' Arms, with the legend:
VIERTE SAECULARFEIER DER
BUCHDRUCKERKUNST.   1440.   1840.

MAYENCE? 1840.

PLÁTE 4 T.

Obverse.—A half-length of Gutenberg holding a book, with half-lengths of Schœffer on his right, and Faust on his left. Legend:

PETER   SCHEFFER   IOHAN   GUTTENBERG
FAUST

In the Exergue:

DEN. 24 IUNI.
1840.

Reverse.—The Printer's Arms, with the legend:

VIERTE SECULARFEIER DER
BUCHDRUCKERKUNST. 1840.

MAYENCE? 1840.

Plate 4 V.

Obverse.—A folio volume, lettered on its side,

>DIE
>HEILIGE
>SCHRIFT.

Over it is

>DAS
>ERSTE BUCH

and beneath is the date

>1440.

The whole surrounded by a wreath of oak-leaves and acorns.

Reverse.—An inscription only:

>ERINNERUNG
>AN DIE
>IV SECULAR FEIER
>DER ERFINDUNG DER
>BUCHDRUKERKUNST
>MDCCCXXXX.

MAYENCE? 1840.

Plate 4 X.

Obverse.—The Thorwaldsen statue of Gutenberg standing alone.

Reverse.—Within a wreath of oak-leaves and acorns, this inscription:

  VIERTES
  SÄCULARFEST
  DER
  ERFINDUNG
  DER
  BUCHDRUCKER :
  KUNST. GEFEIERT
  AM 24$^{T.}$ IUNI
  1840.

There is no engraver's name on either Obverse or Reverse.

PARIS. 1840.

PLATE 4 Y.

Obverse.—The usual profile of Gutenberg, behind which is that of Senefelder, both to the right. Beneath, in small letters, is the name of the designer and engraver,

MONTAGNY

Reverse.—An inscription only:

IMPRIMERIE
GUTTEMBERG
1436

LITHOGRAPHIE
SENEFELDER
1796

This Medal was not struck for sale.

PARIS. 1840.

Plate 4 Z.

Obverse.—A rude Press, on the right side of which is a pair of inking-balls, and upon the left a composing-stick. The legend is:

FUGAT TENEBRAS LUCEMQUE REDUCIT

Above the press, in small letters, is the name of the engraver:

H. STEPH

In the Exergue:

MDCCCXL.

Reverse.—A wreath of oak-leaves and acorns, outside of which is:

ASSOCIATION DES IMPRIMEURS DE PARIS

and inside:

CHAMBRE
DES
IMPRIMEURS

PARIS. 1840.

5 A (See PLATE 4 Z).

Obverse.—The same as the last.

Reverse.—A wreath of oak-leaves and acorns, outside of which is :

ASSOCIATION DES IMPRIMEURS DE PARIS
MDCCCXL.

and inside :

CONFERENCE
DES
IMPRIMEURS.

STRASBOURG. 1840.

PLATE 5 B.

Obverse.—The statue of Gutenberg, erected at Strasbourg in 1840. Guten-

berg is standing upon a pedestal holding out a sheet of paper, upon which is printed

>   ET LA LUMIERE
>   FUT.

At his feet is a small press. Across the field is

>   A JEAN   LA VILLE DE
>   GUTENBERG   STRASBOURG

and, in minute letters, on either side, are the names of the sculptor and of the medallist, viz.,

>   F. J. DAVID D'ANGERS SCULPTEUR.
>   F. KIRSTEIN GRAVEUR.

Reverse.—The Arms of the city of Strasbourg surmounted by a closed helmet and crest of feathers, and supported on either side by a lion statant. The legend is:

>   INVENTION DE L'IMPRIMERIE
>   QUATRIÈME
>   FÊTE SÉCULAIRE
>   24 JUIN 1840

STRASBOURG. 1840.

Plate 5 C.

Obverse.—The bust of Gutenberg to the right, with this legend :

JEAN GUTTENBERG INVENTEUR DE L'IMPRIMERIE

Beneath the bust, in small characters :

G. E. EMMERICK F.

Reverse.—A rude Press, against which is placed a " form" of six pages, and upon which are four books, some sheets of white paper, a pen, and an inkstand. The legend is :

ET LA LUMIERE FUT

In the Exergue is the date,

1440

and to the left the engraver's name as above.

STUTTGART. 1840.

Plate 5 D.

Obverse.—The bust of Gutenberg to the right, around which is :

JOHANNES GUTENBERG

Beneath the bust, in small letters, is the engraver's name :

HEINDEL.

Reverse.—An inscription only :

ZUR IV
SAECULARFEIER
D. ERFINDUNG D.
BUCHDRUCKERKUNST
STUTTGART
MDCCCXL.

This Medal was not struck for sale.

WOLFENBÜTTEL. 1840.

Plate 5 E.

Obverse.—An altar-like structure bearing the inscription :

SÆC. INV. TYPOGR.
CELEBR.

Upon the altar in the centre is the shaft of a pillar bearing a flame upon its apex, and on either side is an open volume; that to the left having the words :

B	A
I	V
B	G

and that to the right :

FE	SPE
REN	RAN
DVM	DVM

Upon the base is the name of the medallist : THIES. The legend is :

ALIIS INSERVIENDO CONSVMOR

and in the Exergue :
>   WOLFENBÜTTEL
>   . MDCCCXL.

Reverse.—The exterior of the library at Wolfenbüttel, and in the Exergue :
>   AMICIS
>   C. SCHÖNEMANN
>   BIBL. AUG. PRÆF

PARIS. 1847.

Plate 5 F.

Obverse.—A mass of clouds, with land and water beneath. Upon the clouds an open printed volume in the full rays of the Sun, over which is a ribbon with the legend :
>   EX UTROQUE LUX

In the Exergue :
>   PARIS.

and Jettons. 99

Reverse.—Arms of the Booksellers of Paris surmounted by a crown, and supported on either side by a sphinx sitting upon a book. The legend: CERCLE DE LA LIBRAIRIE DE L'IMPRIMERIE ET DE LA PAPETERIE. In the Exergue, divided by a large star:
FONDÉ * EN 1847.

NATIONAL PRINTING OFFICE.

Paris, 1848.

PLATE 5 G.

Obverse.—A seated female figure representing France, with rays issuing from her head. Upon her knee she supports with her right hand the Roman fasces, while her left hand rests upon a rudder, against which is a jar bearing the letters s. v. On her right are the gallic cock, a plough, and a wheatsheaf. In front of

her are a Stanhope press, an Alembic, a painter's pallett, and a builder's mallet. The legend is :

> REPUBLIQUE FRANÇAISE

In the Exergue is the date

> 1848

beneath which, in diminutive letters, is :

> E. FAROCHON, D'APRÉS LE SCEAU DE L'ÉTAT.

Reverse.—Within a wreath of oak and laurel leaves the words :

> IMPRIMERIE
> NATIONALE

outside of which is :

> LOIS ADMINISTRATION * SCIENCES
> ET ARTS.

BIRMINGHAM. 1850—60.

5 H (NO PLATE).

Obverse.—Within a double circle :
    M. BILLING
    STEAM
  PRINTING OFFICES
   LIVERY ST.
   BIRMINGHAM.

In small letters :
  COTT   RILL   ST. PAUL'S

Reverse.—Three concentric dotted circles, with space in the middle for a number.

LONDON. c. 1850.

5 I (NO PLATE).

Obverse.—Within a dotted circle :

NISSEN & PARKER
PRINTERS
&
EXPORTING
STATIONERS
43
MARK LANE
LONDON.

Reverse.—In a similar circle :

ACCOUNT BOOKS
ALWAYS
READY.

600 CLASSIFIED
PATTERNS FOR
ALL TRADES,
MANUFACTURES
&
FINANCE.

HAARLEM. 1851.

PLATE 5 K.

Obverse.—The bust of Coster to the left, with a branch of laurel in front, and a branch of oak behind him. Above is the word

HAARLEM

and below, the date

1851

Reverse.—The letter A with wings. The legend is:

TYPOGRAPHIZCHE VEREENIGING TOT NUT
ENGEZEILIG VERKEER.

IMPERIAL PRINTING OFFICE.

Paris, 1854.

Plate 5 L.

Obverse.—The bust of the Emperor Napoleon the Third to the left. Legend:

NAPOLEON III EMPEREUR

and in small letters under the bust, the name of the engraver:

BARRE

Reverse.—A wreath of oak and laurel leaves joined by a bunch of grapes and ears of wheat. In the centre are the words:

IMPRIMERIE
IMPERIALE

and outside the wreath is:

LOIS ADMINISTRATION SCIENCES ET ARTS

BRUSSELS. 1854.

Plate 5 M.

Obverse.—A figure, representing Typography, stands with the right hand resting upon a press, and the left holding a wreath of immortelles. The legend is:
LES OUVRIERS VICTIMES DE LA CONVENTION DU 22 AOUT 1852, RECONNAISSANTS. In the Exergue the date 1854.

Reverse.—Within a heavy wreath of flowers and oak-leaves, the following inscription :
A
F. DEQUICK
J. B. VERBIST
J. LEBON   A. MAHIEU
A. MERTINS
IS. DEMOOR
MEMBRES
DU
COMITÉ CENTRAL TYPOG. BELGE.

DUDLEY. 1856?

5 N (NO PLATE).

Obverse.—Dudley Castle in a small circle, around which is the legend:

HENRY HARPER
PRINTER & MAKER OF
TOKENS CHECKS &c. DUDLEY.

Reverse.—A plain circle, for the insertion of a number.

DUDLEY. 1856?

5 O (NO PLATE).

Obverse.—The Freemasons' sign, a square and compasses, within a double oval, between the lines of which is:
COINS, TOKENS, CHECKS, & PRESSES.
The legend is:
S. HIRON
DIE SINKER
ENGRAVER
DUDLEY
DOOR PLATES.   BRASS SEALS.

Reverse.—A Phœnix rising from the flames. Legend:
PRINTING, STATIONERY,
& BOOKBINDING OFFICE
NEWHALL ST.
DUDLEY.

HAARLEM. 1856.

Plate 5 P.

Obverse.—The statue of Coster erected in the market-place of Haarlem, 1856. The legend is:

DE ORBE MERVIT PATRIA POSVIT

Under the statue:

TYPOGRAPHIAE PATER

and in small letters on the right:

S. G. ELION F.

Reverse.—An allegorical representation of the Sun breaking through the clouds, with the inscription:

DISPVLSIS NEBVLIS
FVLGET
ILLVSTRIOR
INAVG. XVI IVL. MDCCCLVI.

AMSTERDAM. 1857.

PLATE 5 Q.

Obverse.—A Printing-press in the full rays of the sun, with the legend :

TYPOGR. VEREEN. DE NEDERL. DRUKPERS.
1857.

And in very small letters :

B. WOLFF.

Reverse.—Blank, the medal having a ring, and being intended for the breast.

BIRMINGHAM. c. 1860.

5 R (NO PLATE).

Obverse.—A variation of Medal 5 H.

Reverse.—A plain circle for the insertion of a number.

DUDLEY. 1860?

5 S (NO PLATE).

Obverse.—3^{D} in large characters, around which is:

∴ W. HYATT ∴
NEWHALL S^{T}. DUDLEY
CHECK MAKER
& PRINTER

Reverse.—Plain.

SHEFFIELD. 1860.

5 T (NO PLATE).

Obverse.—A Columbian press, above which is
>JOHN BLURTON.

and beneath,
>PRINTER.
>CASTLE STREET
>SHEFFIELD

the whole within a dotted circle.

Reverse.—Britannia seated, her right arm resting upon a shield bearing the National Arms, and her left holding a trident. Behind her is a lion couchant, and before her the ocean, with a ship in full sail. The legend is:
>BRITANNIA PRINTING OFFICE.
>JOHN BLURTON
>CASTLE STREET
>SHEFFIELD
>THE CHEAPEST OFFICE IN THE WORLD.

The whole within a dotted circle.

PARIS. 1860?

Plate 5 V.

Obverse.—An imitation of the Obverse of the small medal by Emmerich, for the Strasbourg Jubilee, 1840 (see Plate 5 B).

Reverse.—Inscription only:
    SOCIÉTÉ
    POUR
    LA POURSUITE
    DES
    CONTREFAÇONS

PARIS. 1861?

5 X.

[See Plate 5 V.]

Obverse.—The same as the last.

Reverse.—Inscription only, in six lines :
SOCIÉTÉ
POUR LA DÉFENSE
DE LA
PROPRIÉTÉ LITTÉRAIRE
ET
ARTISTIQUE

PARIS. 1862.

5 Y (NO PLATE).

Obverse.—A wreath of oak-leaves, outside of which is :

IMPRIMERIE ET LIBRAIRIE CENTRALES
DES CHEMINS DE FER
✶   A. CHAIX & CIE.   ✶

and inside :

COURS
DES
APPRENTIS.

Reverse.—Inscription only :

✶
SI QUELQU'UN VOUS DIT
QUE VOUS POUVEZ VOUS ENRICHIR
AUTREMENT QUE PAR LE TRAVAIL
ET L'ÉCONOMIE,
NE L'ÉCOUTEZ PAS,
C'EST UN EMPOISONNEUR.
FRANKLIN

MANCHESTER. 1863?

5 Z (NO PLATE).

Obverse.—The head of the Queen to the left, imitated from the coinage. The legend is:

VICTORIA QUEEN OF GREAT BRIT :

The whole within a circle of beads.

Reverse.—
* WILLIAM SHAW *
STATIONER
& PRINTER
. MANCHESTER

The whole within a circle of beads.

LONDON. 1863.

Plate 6 A.

Obverse.—The head of Alex. Herzen, with profile to the right, beneath which is the engraver's name:

CH. WIENER

Legend :

ALEXANDER HERZEN

Reverse.—A Bell, upon the top of which, in Sclavonic characters, is :

ZEMLO E BOLO

and upon the edge of which is :

VIVOS VOCO.

To the left is the year 1853, and to the right 1863. The legend is :

FIRST DECENIUM OF THE FREE RUSSIAN PRESS IN LONDON.

PARIS. 1866.

6 B (no plate).

Obverse.—A Bee-hive in full activity, under which is:

* PARIS-CLICHY *
1866

Legend:
IMPRIMERIE DE PAUL DUPONT
OMNIA LABORE

Reverse.—Two right hands clasped together; beneath, in small letters:

*
CAQUÉ

Legend:
SOCIÉTÉ DE SECOURS MUTUELS
*
DECERNÉE
À

(space for a name).

BIRMINGHAM. 1868.

6 C (NO PLATE).

Obverse.—The following inscription only :

    BILLING BRO^S
    PRINTERS &c.
    ———◆———
    11
    S^T PAULS SQ^R
    BIRMINGHAM.

Reverse.—A simple ring near the edge, the centre being left blank for the insertion of a name or number.

SUPPLEMENT.

THERE are certain Medals which, although struck for men who were sometime Printers, do not in any way refer to their connection with that art. These cannot perhaps, strictly speaking, be called Printers' Medals, nor on the other hand should they be entirely omitted from a list like this. The following are the only specimens of this class that have come under my notice; but there are doubtless others, information concerning which will be welcomed by the Author.

ALBERT DURER. Many medals have been struck in honour of this artist, who was a letter-press printer for many years before his death. He himself engraved a beautiful medallion of his wife AGNES, who as a widow continued the Printing-office for at least two years after her husband's death.

BENJAMIN FRANKLIN. At least fourteen medals have been issued in memory of Franklin the Politician, the Patriot, and the man of Science; but, so far as I can learn, not one has commemorated the fact most interesting to us—that he was a famous Printer.

JOHN GOUGH NICHOLS, F.S.A., &c. A medal in memory of the silver wedding of this well-known London Printer was struck in 1868.

BÉRANGER the French poet was, for a period of his youth, a working Printer. Has any medal of this poet been struck?

INDEX.

A, the letter, with wings, 103.
Aldus Pius Manutius, 1.
Alexandri grammatica, 32.
Aliis inserviendo, &c., 97.
Als Gutenberg und Faust, &c., 19.
Altdorf, Medal, 17.
Amsterdam, Medals, 7, 11, 109.
Anchor and Dolphin, 1.
Andrieu, Medallist, 50.
Anspach, Medal, 17.
Arms :—
  Amsterdam, 11.
  Bath, 42.
  Baumgarten, 49.
  Booksellers and Printers of Paris, 15, 99.
  Cologne, 77.
  Gutenberg family, 23, 76.
  Haarlem, 13, 24, 27, 28, 32, 55,
  Burgomasters of Haarlem, 24.
Arms :
  Leyden, 10.
  Lyons, 85.
  Mayence, 20, 77, 83.
  North Holland, 55.
  Nuremberg, 37, 40.
  Printers of Germany, 19, 76, 87, 88.
  Ratisbon, 41.
  Strasbourg, 77.
  Verona, 16.
Ars victura dum, &c., 34.
Arte et marte, 12.
Arte sua litteras auxit, 70.
Artem quæ Græcos, &c., 62.
Arti typographicæ a Io. Guttenbergio, &c., 14.
Association des Imp. de Paris, 92, 93.
Audi, vide, et tace, 5.
Augsburg, Medals, 62, 70, 77.
Aurora, 14.
Auspicio Imperii summæ decus, &c., 36.
Ayrer, U. M., 71.

Bamberg, Medals, 71, 72.
Basle, Medals, 18, 73.
Barre, Medallist, 104.
Bath, Medals, 42, 43.
Baumann, G., 5.
Baumgarten, 49.
Beehive, 117.
Beneficio Dei et solertia, &c., 37.
Benevolence, Figure of, 42.
Béranger, the poet, 120.
Berlin, Medals, 63, 64, 74, 75, 76.
Billing Bros., Birmingham, 118.
Billing, M., 101, 109.
Binder's Press, 7, 11.
Birmingham, Medals, 101, 109, 118.
Blurton, John, 111.
Bodoni, J. B., 48.
Boucherono, Chas., 68.
Bovy, A., Medallist, 73.
Braemt, Medallist, 55.
Breslau, Medals, 5, 19, 49.
Britannia Printing Office, 111.
Brussels, Medal, 105.

Caqué, 117.

Civi optimo decurioni, &c., 48.
Chaix et Cie., Paris, 114.
Clichy, 117.
Cologne, Medal, 77.
Columbian Press, 111.
Comes Consiliorum, 13.
Coster, 24, 26, 27, 29, 31, 32, 55, 57, 103, 108.
Cottrill, Medallist, 101.

D. V. & Z., 56.
Dam. capt. Typ. inv., &c., 12.
Damietta, 8, 24.
D'Angers, F. J. D., Sculptor, 94.
Das erste buch, 89.
Das ist vom Herrn, &c., 75.
Dassier, J., Medallist, 35.
De orbe meruit, &c., 108.
Decus urbis et artis, 41.
De Drukkunst nu, 26.
Dem andenken Alb. Pfisters, 71.
Demoor, J., 105.
Denton, J., 46.
Deo opt. max., &c., 38.
Depaulis, Medallist, 60.
Dequick, F., 105.

Der Welt die Warheit, 76.
Didot, Firmin, 69.
" Jules, 54.
" Pierre, 54.
Digna viro pro talibus ausis, 21.
Dispulsis Nebulis, &c., 108.
Dissimulare hunc virum, &c., 23, 70.
Donatus gram. quid, 55.
Dresden, Medal, 20.
Dudley, 106, 107, 110.
Dudley Castle, 106.
Dupont et Cie., 61, 117.
Durand, Editor, 51.
Durer, Albert, 119.
" Agnes, 119.

Eaton, D. I., 45.
Ehrhardt, Medallist, 83.
Elion, S. G., Medallist, 108.
Elsevier, Abraham, 10.
Emmerick, G. E., Medallist, 95, 112.
Erfuhrt, Medal, 20.
Et la lumiere fut, 94, 95.
Ex his tibi necte coronam, 32.
Ex utroque lux, 15, 98.

Farochon, E., Medallist, 100.
Faust, John, 19, 34, 37, 78, 84, 87, 88.
Felici fœdere crescunt, 21.
Felix Germania, 36.
Felix inventum Germaniæ, 33.
Ferendum sperandum, 97.
Festival in 1740 :—
  Altdorf, 17.
  Anspach, 17.
  Basle, 18.
  Breslau, 19.
  Dresden, 20.
  Erfuhrt, 20.
  Gotha, 22.
  Gottingen, 23.
  Haarlem, 24—32.
  Leipsig, 33, 34.
  Nuremberg, 35—40.
  Ratisbon, 41.
Festival in 1823 :—
  Haarlem, 55—58.
Festival in 1837 :—
  Augsburg, 62.
  Berlin, 63, 64.
  Mayence, 65.
Festival in 1840 :—
  Augsburg, 70.
  Bamberg, 71, 72.

Festival in 1840 :—
  Basle, 73.
  Berlin, 74—76.
  Cologne, 77.
  Frankfort, 78.
  Leipsig, 79—84.
  Lyons, 85, 86.
  Mayence, 87—90.
  Paris, 91—93.
  Strasbourg, 94, 95.
  Stuttgart, 96.
  Wolfenbüttel, 97.
Festival in 1856 :—
  Haarlem, 108.
Frankfurt, 77, 78.
Franklin, Benj., 114, 120.
Franklin Press, 44.
Frobenius, Joh., 73.
Fugat tenebras, 92.
Fust, John (*see* Faust).

Gaensfleisch, 77.
Gaudet Verona, &c., 16.
Gayrard, Medallist, 51.
Gensfleisch, 63, 65.
Ghertzen (see Herzen).
Giraud, Medallist, 66.
Gloria Germanorum, &c., 39.
Go forth, 42.
Goethen, Peter van, 7.

Gotha, Medals, 14, 22.
Gottingen, Medal, 23.
Grass and Barth, 49.
Gutenberg, John, 19, 20, 23, 32, 34, 37, 51, 61—65, 70, 74, 76—81, 83, 86—88, 90, 91, 93—96.
Gutenberg, His Arms, 76.
Gye, W., 42.

Haarlem, Medals, 8, 9, 12, 13, 24—33, 55—58, 103, 108.
Hamelburg, 73.
Harper, Henry, 106.
Heden my morghen dy, 6.
Heindel, Medallist, 96.
Herzen, Alexander, 116.
Hinc totum sparguntur, &c., 31.
Hiron, S., 107.
Holtzhey, Engraver, 25, 26.
Horace, 54.
Hyatt, W., 110.

Ich dien, 47.
I. F., 19.
I. G., 19.
Imperial Printing Office, Paris, 104.

Index. 125

Insignia. gentilit., &c., 23.
Inventori artis Typographicae, 63.

JAH, 36.

Kirstein, F., Medallist, 94.
König, Medallist, 74.
Koster (*see* Coster).
Kruger, Medallist, 76.

L L S, 41.
Lafontaine, 54.
Lambeth, 46, 47.
Lambeth Palace, 47.
Lange Lévy et Cie., 67.
Laus Urbi, lux Orbi, 55.
Lebon, J., 105.
Leipsig, Medals, 33, 34, 79—83.
— University, 35.
Les ouvriers victimes, &c., 105.
Leyden, Medal, 10.
Lille, Medal, 9.
Lois administration, &c., 100, 104.
London, Medals, 44, 45, 102, 116.
Loos, G., Medallist, 63, 74.

Lorenz, B., Medallist, 63.
Louis Philippe, 60.
Lugdun (*see* Lyons).
Lumen ad revelationem, 66.
Lyons, Medals, 85, 86.
— Arms of, 85.

Mahieu, A., 105.
Manchester, Medal, 115.
Manfredini, L., 48.
Marshoorn, G., 27, 28.
Mayence, Medals, 65, 81, 87—90.
— Arms of, 20, 77, 83.
Medallists :—
 Andrieu, 50.
 Barre, 104.
 Bovy, A., 73.
 Braemt, 55.
 Dassier, J., 35.
 Depaulis, 60.
 De Vries and Zoon, 56.
 Ehrhardt, 83.
 Elion, S. G., 108.
 Emmerick, G. E., 95, 112.
 Farochon, E., 100.
 Gayrard, 51.
 Heindel, 96.
 Holtzhey, M., 25, 26.

Medallists:—
　Kirstein, F., 94.
　König, 74.
　Kruger, 76.
　Loos, G., 63, 74.
　Manfredini, 48.
　Marshoorn, G., 27, 28.
　Montagny, 91.
　Neuss, I. I., 62, 70, 71.
　Nürnberger, 39.
　Perrin, 86.
　Steph, H., 92.
　Swindern, N. Van, 31, 32.
　Thies, 97.
　Vestner, 36.
　Veyrat, 54.
　Wartig, 81.
　Werner, 21.
　Wolff, B., 109.
Medusa's head, 10, 21, 70.
Memor. fel., &c., 23.
Mentelin, 37.
Mercury, 11, 18.
Mertins, A., 105.
Mey, Jan de, 6.
Middleburg, Medal, 6.
Minerva, 10, 21, 25, 38.
Montagny, Medallist, 91.

Napoleon I., 50, 60.

Napoleon III., 104.
National Printing Office, Paris, 99.
Neuss, I. I., Medallist, 62, 70, 71.
Nichols, John Gough, 120.
Nissen and Parker, 102.
North Holland, Arms of, 55.
Novas mirabitur artes, 33.
Nuremberg, Medals, 2, 35—40.
Nürnberger, Medallist, 39.

Omnia labore, 117.

P. D. (Paul Dupont), 61.
Pancoucke, C. L. F., Medal by, 53.
Paris, Booksellers' Arms, 99.
— Cercle de la Librairie, &c., 99.
— Imperial Printing Office, 50, 104.
— Medals, 3, 4, 15, 50—54, 59—61, 66, 67, 91—93, 98, 99, 104, 112—114, 117.
— National Printing Office, 99.

Index.

Paris, Royal Printing Office, 59, 60.
— Société pour la poursuite des contrefaçons, 112.
— Société pour la defense de la propriété, 113.
Parma, 48.
Penin, Medallist, 86.
Per tria secula, 31.
Pernecker, J., 71.
Petreius, John, 2.
Petzensteiner, H., 71.
Pfeil, J., 71.
Pfister, Albert, 71.
Pig-stye, 45.
Pomba, J., 68.
Prince of Wales, feathers, 47.

Racine, 54.
Ratisbon, Medal, 41.
Regiomontanus, 37.
Remember the debtors of Ilchester Goal, 42.
Rerum tutissima custos, 18.
Reyherorum Officina, 22.
Roman, Zachs., 6.
Royal Printing Office, Paris, 59, 60.
Russian Free Press, 116.

Sacra Dei honori, &c., 41.
Schœffer, Peter, 37, 63, 78, 84, 87, 88.
Schönemann, C., 98.
Schreck, publisher, 81.
Senatus consulto, 8, 13.
Senefelder, 61, 86, 91.
Sensenschmidt, J., 71.
Sermo Dei ignitus, &c., 2.
Series Numismatica Virorum illustrium, 51.
Servandis artibus una, 85.
Shaw, William, Printers' ticket, 115.
Sheffield, Medal, 111.
Sic oritur doctrina, 44.
Sie gaben macht, &c., 87.
Spare, the river, 12.
Speculum humani salvationis, 29.
Spes O fidissima Musis, 33.
ΣΠΕΥΔΕ ΒΡΑΔΕΩΣ, 1.
Spiegel onser behoudenisse, 24, 28.
Sporer, H., 71.
St. John the Evangelist, 3, 4.
Stanhope Press, 100.
Steph, H., Medallist, 92.
Stephanorum æmulus, &c., 69.

Strasbourg, Medals, 93, 112.
— Arms of, 94.
Stuttgart, Medal, 96.
Swindern, Van, Medallist, 30, 31.

Tebays, W., 42.
Thies, Medallist, 97.
Thorwaldsen Statue on Medals, 62—65, 70, 79, 90.
Tuis hic omnia plena, 36.
Turin, Medal, 68.
Typogr. Vereen, &c., 109.
Typographia hic primum inventa, 25.
Typographiæ pater, 108.
Typographizche Vereeniging, &c., 103.

Und es ward licht, 77.
Ut aurora musis amica, 14.

Venice, 1.
Verbist, J. B., 105.
Vestner, Medallist, 36.
Verona, Medal, 16.
Veyrat, Medallist, 54.
Vicit vim virtus, 8, 13.
Virgil, 54.
Vivos voco, 116.
Volpi, John Antony, 16.

Wante, Paul, 6.
Wartig, Medallist, 81.
Werner, Medallist, 21.
Wilmerdonx, John, 7.
Wolfenbüttel, Medal, 97.
Wolff, B., Medallist, 109.

Pl. A.

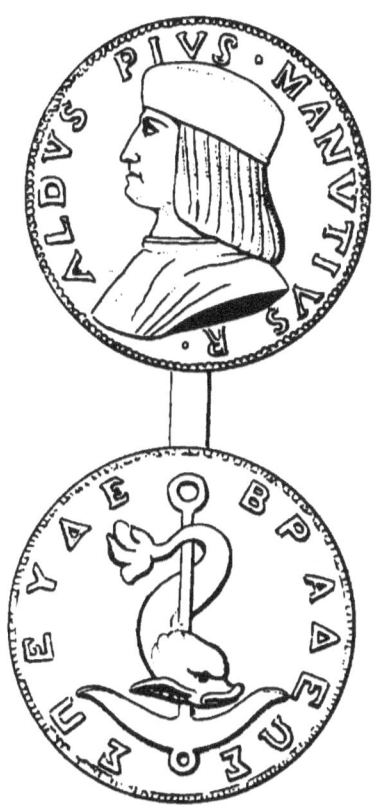

Pl. B.

Pl. C.

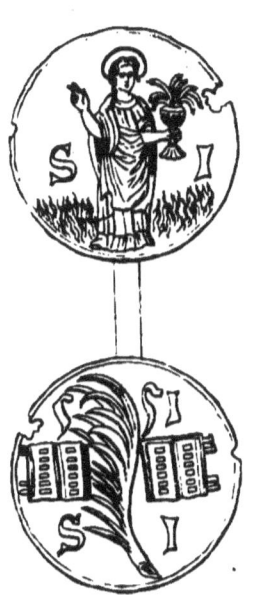

Pl. D.

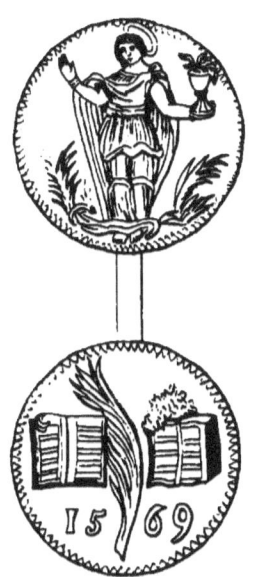

Pl. F.

Pl. G.

Pl. H.

Pl. I.

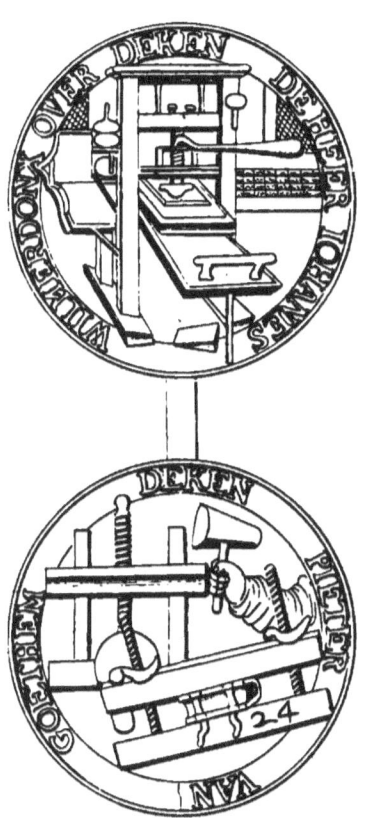

Pl. K.

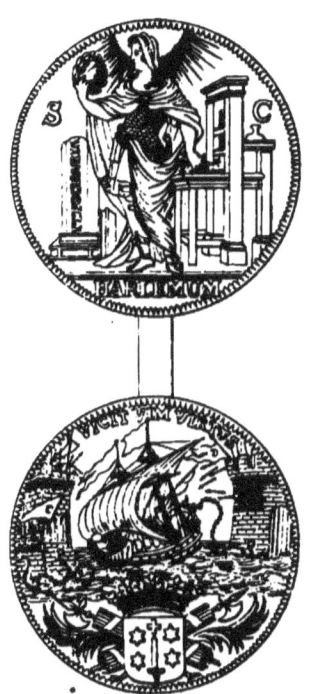

Pl. L.

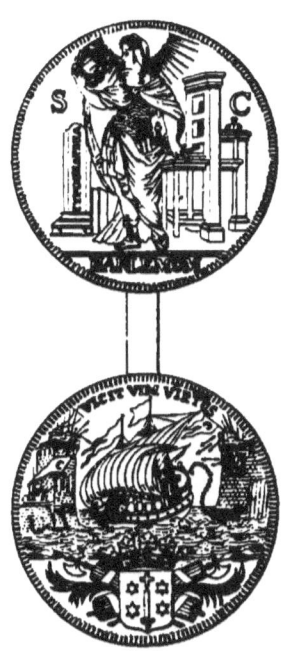

Pl. M.

Pl. N.

Pl. O.

Pl. P.

Pl. R.

Pl. S.

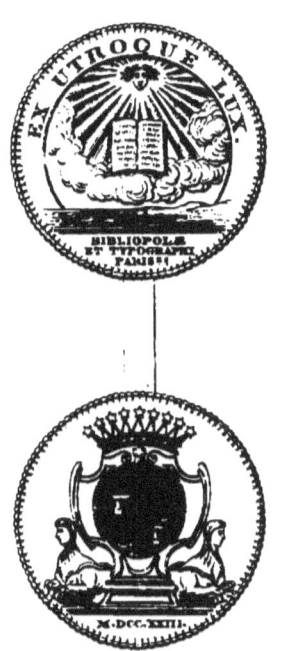

Pl. T.

Pl. Y.

REFERENTISSIMA
CUSTOS

ARTIS TYPOGR.
SACRIS SÆCULAR.
III
AUGUST. RAURAC.
FELICITER CELEBR.
A · S · MDCCXI ·

Pl. Z.

Pl. 2.B.

Pl. 2 C.

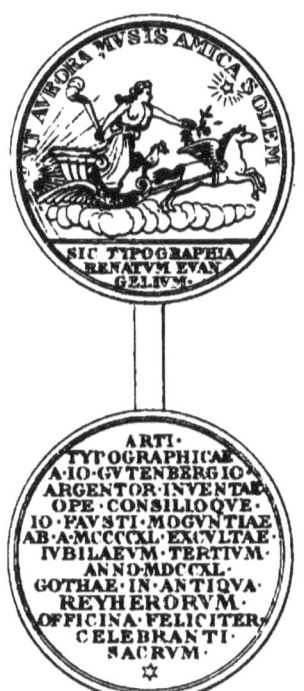

Pl. 2.D.

Pl. 2.F.

Pl. 2. H.

Pl. 2.I.

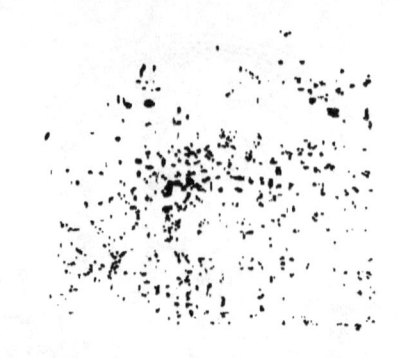

Pl. 2.K.

Pl. 2.L.

Pl. 2.M.

Pl. 2.N.

Pl. 20.

Pl. 2.P.

Pl. 2. Q.

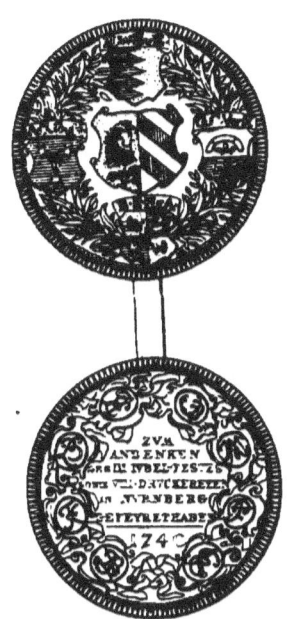

Pl. 2.R.

Pl. 2.T.

Pl. 2. U.

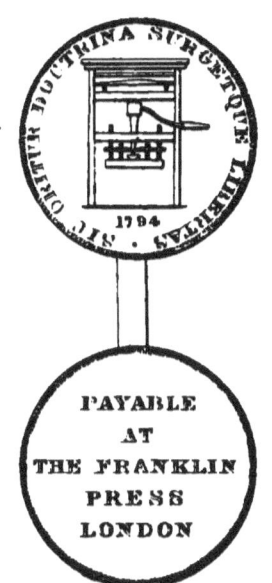

Pl. 2.X.

Pl. 2. Y.
Pl. 2. Z.
Pl. 3. A.

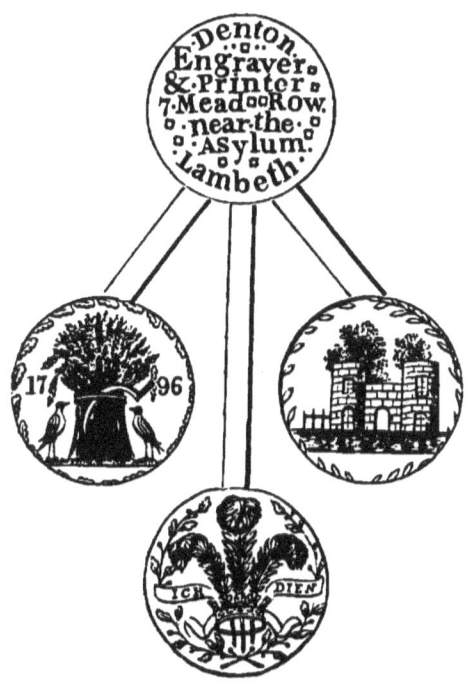

Pl. 3.B.

Pl. 3.C.

Pl. 3.D.

Pl. 3.E.

Pl. 3.F.

Pl. 3. H.

Pl. 3.I.

Pl. 3K.

Pl. 3.L.

Pl. 3. N.

Pl. 30.

Pl. 3.P.

Pl. 3. Q.

Pl. 3.R.

MON·IO·GVTTENBERGII·P·M·D·XIV·AVG· MDCCCXXXVII·MOGVNTIAE·POS·

ARTEM
QVAE GRAECOS LATVIT,
LATVITQVE LATINOS,
GERMANI SOLERS
EXTVDIT INGENIVM.
NVNC QVIDQVID
VETERES SAPIVNT,
SAPIVNTQVE RECENTES,
NON SIBI,
SED POPVLIS OMNIBVS
ID SAPIVNT.

Pl. 3.S.

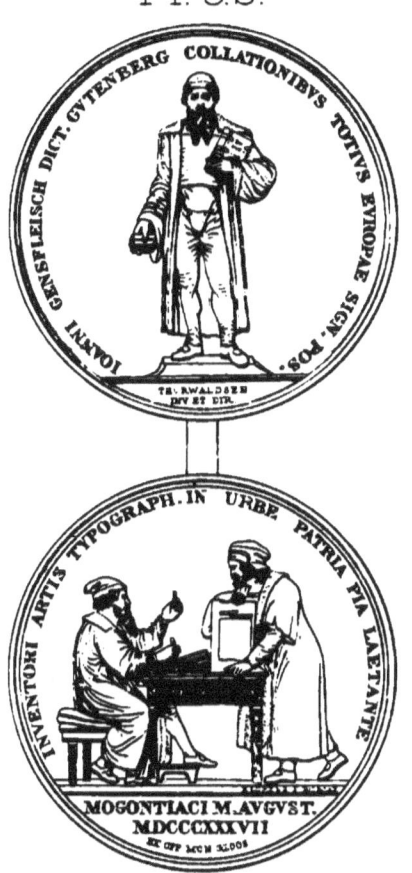

Pl. 3.T.

Pl. 3.X.

Pl. 3. Y.

Pl. 3.Z.

Pl. 4A.

Pl. 4.B.

Pl. 4.C.

Pl. 4.E.

Pl. 4. F.

Pl. 4.G.

Pl. 4H.

Pl. 41.

Pl.4.K.

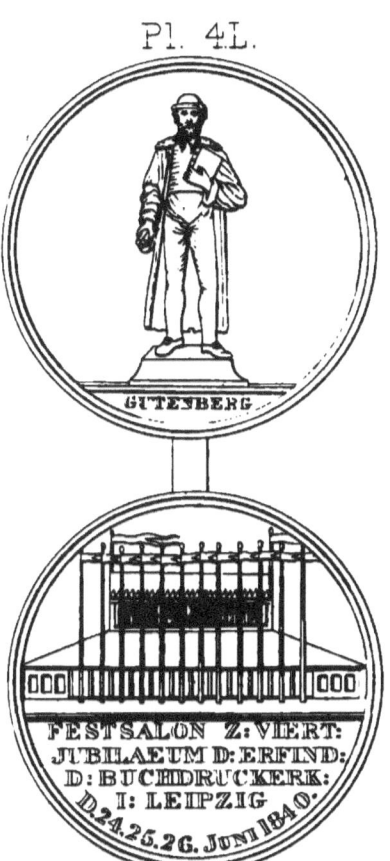

Pl. 4L.

Pl. 4. M.

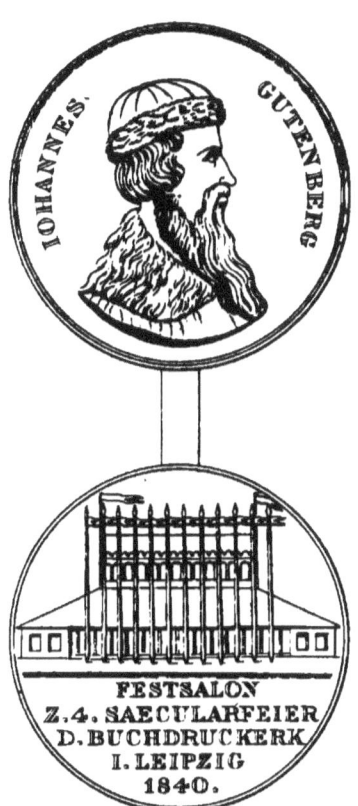

Pl. 4. N.

Pl. 4. P.

Pl. 4.Q.

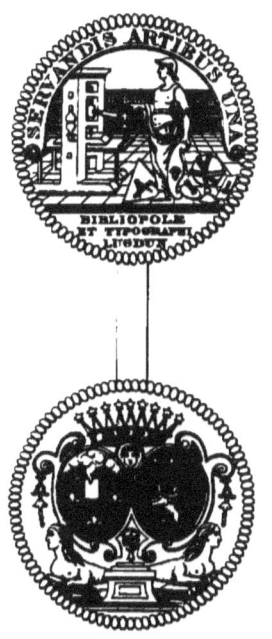

Pl. 4. R.

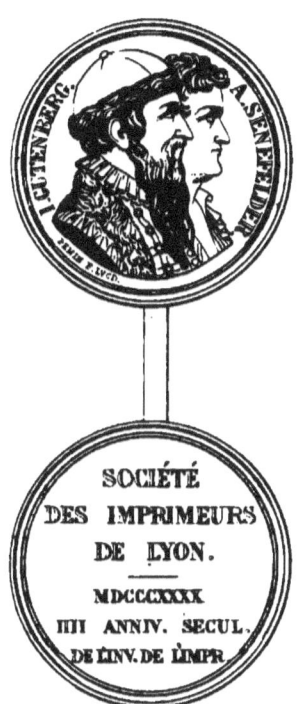

Pl. 4. S.

Pl. 4. T.

Pl. 4. V.

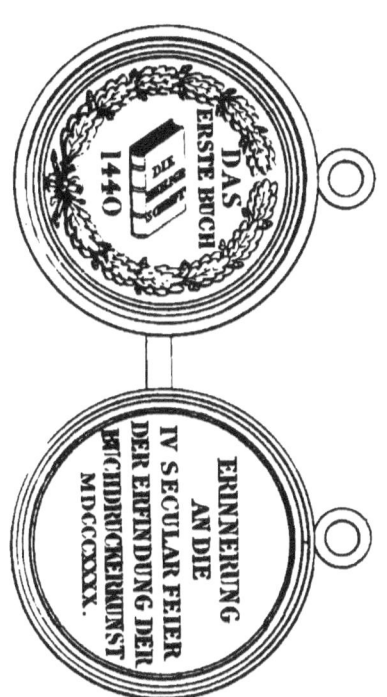

Pl. 4.X.

Pl. 4. Y.

Pl. 4. Z.

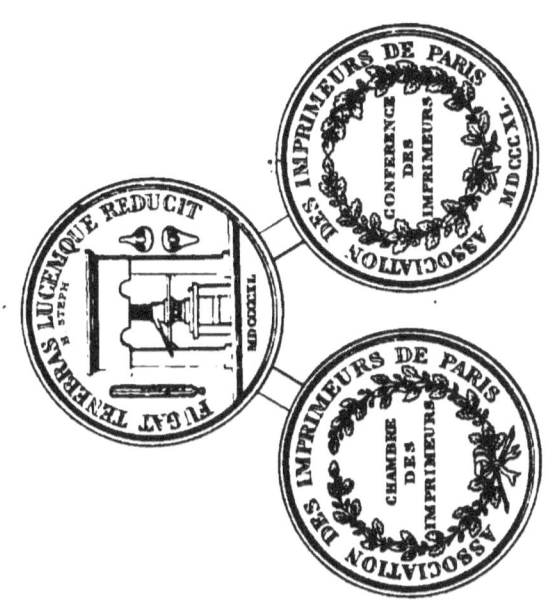

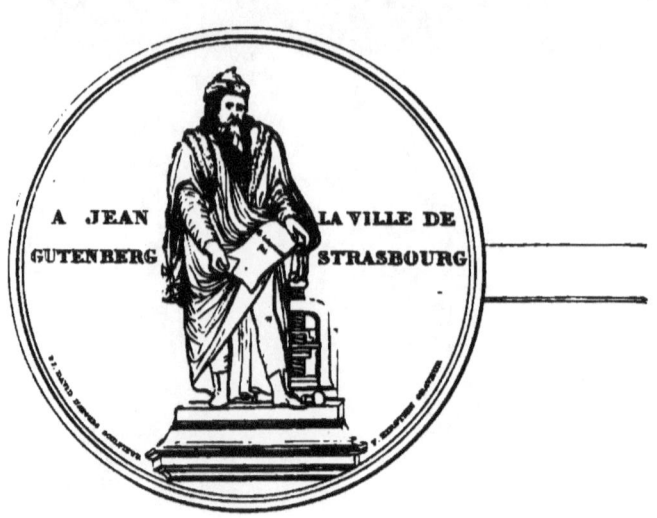

Pl. 5. C.

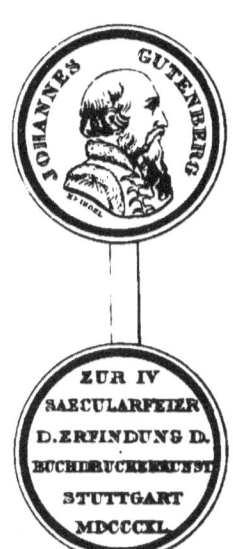

Pl. 5. E.

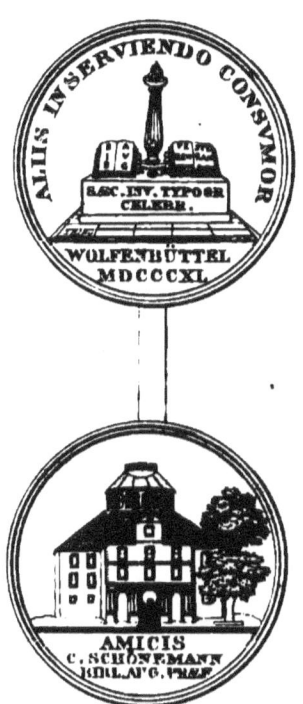

Pl. 5.F.

Pl. 5. G.

Pl. 5.L.

Pl. 5. M.

Pl. 5. N.

Pl. **5**. Q.

Pl. 5. V.

Pl. 6.A.

L234
B62

DESIDERATA.

M. BLADES, 11, Abchurch Lane, London, demande les Médailles ci-dessous décrites:—

Nota.—Les Numéros renvoyent à la " List of Printers' Medals and Jettons," par M. Blades, 8vo., London, 1869.

Page. Pl.
1. A. *Av.* Buste d' " Aldus Pius Manutius."
2. B. *Av.* Buste de " Ioh. Petreius, Typographus."
5. F. *Av.* Buste de " Georg. Bawman, Typographus."
6. H. *Av.* Zacharias Roman.
    Rev. " Heden my morghen dy 1631."
10. N. *Av.* Minerve. " Acad-Lvgd. Batav."
    Rev. " Abrahamvs Elscvirivs 1652."
16. T. *Av.* Buste de I. A. Vulpius.
    Rev. " Gaudet Verona," &c., 1737.

Le Jubilé de 1740.

17. V. Altdorf.
    X. Anspach.
18. Y. Basle (Augst).
    Av. Mercure. Une presse typographique. Rerum tutissima Custos.
    Rev. Inscription seulement : " Artis Typogr.," &c.
20. 2A. Dresden.
    Av. " Mein eintzger Schein "
    " Dringt vielmahl ein."
    Rev. " Gottes Seegen und Gedeyen "
    " Wird uns fernerweit erfreuen."
20. 2B. Erfurt.
    Av. Buste de Gutenberg sur un piédestal. Quatre livres avec leurs titres : " Digna Viro, &c.
    Rev. Minerve et la Typographie, le bouclier et le hibou : " Felici Fœdere," &c. Werner fecit Erford.
22. 2C. Gotha.
    Av. " Ut Aurora Musis amica Solem, &c.
23. 2D. *Av.* Inscription de 12 lignes commençant " Mœmor. fel. Jo. Guttenberg " et finisant : " Aere Modico Parare."
    Rev. Armoiries de la famille de Guttenberg. " Dissimulare hunc Virum &c.
27. 2G. Haarlem. Le " Grand Marshoorn."

Page. Pl.
38. 2P. Nuremberg.
Av. Un Vieillard dans les nuages. Minerve avec un phylactère. Quatre génies avec des instruments typographiques. "Gloria Germanorum &c.
Rev. Inscription: " D. G. Iubilæum Tertium" &c.

41. 2R. Ratisbonne.
Av. Armoires de la Ville. "Decus urbis et artis."
Rev. " Sacra dei honori."

---

49. 3C. Grass et Barth, Breslau, 1804.
Av. Un Lion, un Aigle, 1504.
Rev. " Dreihundertiahriges," &c.

61. 3Q. Un jetton octogone de P. Dupont et Cie., 1836 ?
66. 3X. Un jetton, " Fonderie générale de caractères française et étrangère, 1837."
67. 3Y. Un jetton octogone de Lange Lévy et Cie., 1837.
68. 3Z. Turin.
Av. Buste de "Carolo Boucherono," J. Pomba, Typ., 1837.

Le Jubilé de 1840.

78. 4K. Francfort.
Av. Le monument des trois imprimeurs.
Rev. " Zu ehren," &c.

85. 4Q. Médaille des " Bibliopolæ et Typographi Lugdun."
86. 4R. Jetton de la " Société des Imprimeurs, Lyon."
89. 4V. Mayence ?
Av. Un livre. " Das erste buch."
Rev. " Erinnerung an die," &c.

91. 4Y. Paris. Médaille de Montagny. Les bustes de Gutenberg et Senefelder.

---

92. 4Z. Jetton pour la " Chambre des Imprimeurs" de Paris.
93. 5A. Jetton pour la " Conférence des Imprimeurs" de Paris.
109. 5Q. Amsterdam, 1857. " Typogr. Vereen. de Nederl. Drukpers."
112. 5V. Paris. Société pour la poursuite des contrefaçons.
113. 5Y. Paris. Société pour la défense de la propriété litt.
114. 5Y. Jetton A. Chaix et Cie. "Cours des apprentis."
117. 6B. Jetton Paul Dupont. Société de secours mutuel.

Cette Liste est destinée d'être détachée de la touche, et l'auteur prie avec instances de la faire circuler parmi les Imprimeurs, les Numismates, et les Amateurs.

DESIDERATA.

M. BLADES, 11, Abchurch Lane, London, demande les Médailles ci-dessous décrites :—

Nota.—Les Numéros renvoyent à la "List of Printers' Medals and Jettons," par M. Blades, 8vo., London, 1869.

Page. Pl.
1. A. *Av.* Buste d' "Aldus Pius Manutius."
2. B. *Av.* Buste de " Ioh. Petreius, Typographus."
5. F. *Av.* Buste de " Georg. Bawman, Typographus."
6. H. *Av.* Zacharias Romian.
   Rev. " Heden my morghen dy 1681."
10. N. *Av.* Minerva " Acad-Lwgd. Batav."
    Rev. " Abrahamvs Elsevirivs 1652."
16. T. *Av.* Buste de I. A. Vulpius.
    Rev. " Gaudet Verona," &c., 1737.

Le Jubilé de 1740.

17. V. Altdorf.
    X. Anspach.
18. Y. Basle (Augst).
    Av. Mercure. Une presse typographique. "Rerum totissima Castes.
    Rev. Inscription seulement : " Artis Typogr.," &c.
20. 2A. Dresden.
    Av. " Mein einziger Schein."
         " Dringt vielmahl ein,"
    Rev. " Gottes Seegen und Gedeyen "
         " Wird uns fernerweit erfreuen."
20. 2B. Erfurt.
    Av. Buste de Gutenberg sur un piédestal. Quatre livres avec leurs titres : " Digna Viro, &c."
    Rev. Minerve et la Typographie, le bouclier et le hibou : " Felici Foedere," &c. Werner fecit Erford.
22. 2C. Gotha.
    Av. " Ut Aurora Musis amica Solem, &c.
23. 2D. *Av.* Inscription de 12 lignes commençant " Mœmor. fel: Jo. Guttenberg" et finisant : " Xere Modico Parare."
    Rev. Armoiries de la famille de Guttenberg. " Dissimulare hunc Virum &c.
27. 2G. Haarlem. Le " Grand Marshoorn."

Page.	Pl.	
38.	2P.	Nuremberg.

Av. Un Vieillard dans les nuages. Minerve avec un phylactère. Quatre génies avec des instruments typographiques. "Gloria Germanorum &c."
Rev. Inscription : " D. G. Iubilæum Tertium" &c.

41. 2R. Ratisbonne.
Av. Armoires de la Ville. "Decus urbis et artis."
Rev. " Sacra dei honori."

49. 3C. Grass et Barth, Breslau, 1804.
Av. Un Lion, un Aigle, 1504.
Rev. " Dreihundertjahriges," &c.

61. 3Q. Un jetton octogone de P. Dupont et Cie., 1836 ?

66. 3X. Un jetton, " Fonderie générale de caractères française et étrangère, 1837."

67. 3Y. Un jetton octogone de Lange Lévy et Cie., 1837.

68. 3Z. Turin.
Av. Buste de " Carolo Boucherono," J. Pomba, Typ., 1837.

Le Jubilé de 1840.

78. 4K. Francfort.
Av. Le monument des trois imprimeurs.
Rev. " Zu chren," &c.

85. 4Q. Médaille des " Bibliopolæ et Typographi Lugduni."

86. 4R. Jetton de la " Société des Imprimeurs, Lyon."

89. 4V. Mayence ?
Av. Un livre. " Das erste buch."
Rev. " Erinnerung an die," &c.

91. 4Y. Paris. Médaille de Montagny. Les bustes de Gutenberg et Senefelder.

92. 4Z. Jetton pour la " Chambre des Imprimeurs " de Paris.

93. 5A. Jetton pour la " Conférence des Imprimeurs " de Paris.

109. 5Q. Amsterdam, 1857. Typogr. Vereen. de Nederl. Drukpers.

112. 5V. Paris. Société pour la poursuite des contrefaçons.

113. 5Y. Paris. Société pour la défense de la propriété litt.

114. 5Y. Jetton A. Chaix et Cie. " Cours des apprentis."

117. 6B. Jetton Paul Dupont. Société de secours mutuel.

Cette Liste est destinée d'être détachée de la touche, et l'auteur prie avec instances de la faire circuler parmi les Imprimeurs, les Numismates, et les Amateurs.

DESIDERATA.

M. BLADES, 11, Abchurch Lane, London, demande les Médailles ci-dessous décrites:—

Nota.—Les Numéros renvoyent à la " List of Printers' Medals and Jettons," par M. Blades, 8vo., London, 1869.

Page. Pl.
1. A. *Av.* Buste d' " Aldus Pius Manutius."
2. B. *Av.* Buste de " Ioh. Petreius, Typographus."
5. F. *Av.* Buste de " Georg. Bawman, Typographus."
6. H. *Av.* Zacharias Romian.
   Rev. " Heden my morghen dy 1631."
10. N. *Av.* Minerve. " Acad-Lvgd. Batav."
    Rev. " Abrahamvs Elsevirivs 1652.
16. T. *Av.* Buste de I. A. Vulpius.
    Rev. " Gaudet Verona," &c., 1737.

Le Jubilé de 1740.

17. V. Altdorf.
    X. Anspach.
18. Y. Basle (Augst).
    Av. Mercure. Une presse typographique. " Rerum tutissimus Custos.
    Rev. Inscription seulement : " Artis Typogr.," &c.
20. 2A. Dresden.
    Av. " Mein einiger Schein."
    " Dringt vielmahl ein."
    Rev. " Gottes Seegen und Gedeyen "
    " Wird uns fernerwelt erfreuen."
20. 2B. Erfurt.
    Av. Buste de Gutenberg sur un piédestal. Quatre livres avec leurs titres: " Digna Vigo, &c."
    Rev. Minerve et la Typographie, le bouclier et le hibou: " Felici Foedere," &c. Werner fecit Erford.
22. 2C. Gotha.
    Av. " Ut Aurora Musis amica Solem, &c.
23. 2D. *Av.* Inscription de 12 lignes commençant " Mœmor. fel. Jo. Guttenberg" et finisant: " Aere Modico Pararo."
    Rev. Armoiries de la famille de Guttenberg. " Dissimulare hunc Virum &c.
27. 2G. Haarlem. Le " Grand Marshoorn."

Page.	Pl.	
38.	2P.	Nuremberg. *Av.* Un Vieillard dans les nuages. Minerve avec un phylactère. Quatre génies avec des instruments typographiques. "Gloria Germanorum &c." *Rev.* Inscription: "D. G. Iubilæum Tertium" &c.
41.	2R.	Ratisbonne. *Av.* Armoires de la Ville. "Decus urbis et artis." *Rev.* "Sacra dei honori."
49.	3C.	Grass et Barth, Breslau, 1804. *Av.* Un Lion, un Aigle, 1504. *Rev.* "Dreihundertiahriges," &c.
61.	3Q.	Un jetton octogone de P. Dupont et Cie., 1836 ?
66.	3X.	Un jetton, "Fonderie générale de caractères française et étrangère, 1837."
67.	3Y.	Un jetton octogone de Lange lévy et Cie., 1837.
68.	3Z.	Turin. *Av.* Buste de "Carolo Boucherono," J. Pomba, Typ., 1837.

Le Jubilé de 1840.

78.	4K.	Francfort. *Av.* Le monument des trois imprimeurs. *Rev.* "Zu ehren," &c.
85.	4Q.	Médaille des "Bibliopolæ et Typographi Lugdun."
86.	4R.	Jetton de la "Société des Imprimeurs, Lyon."
89.	4V.	Mayence? *Av.* Un livre. "Das erste buch." *Rev.* "Erinnerung an die," &c.
91.	4Y.	Paris. Médaille de Montagny. Les bustes de Gutenberg et Senefelder.
92.	4Z.	Jetton pour la "Chambre des Imprimeurs" de Paris.
93.	5A.	Jetton pour la "Conférence des Imprimeurs" de Paris.
109.	5Q.	Amsterdam, 1857. "Typogr. Vereen, de Nederl. Drukpers.
112.	5V.	Paris. Société pour la poursuite des contrefaçons.
113.	5Y.	Paris. Société pour la défense de la propriété litt.
114.	5Y.	Jetton A. Chaix et Cie. "Cours des apprentis."
117.	6B.	Jetton Paul Dupont. Société de secours mutuel.

DESIDERATA.

M. BLADES, 11, Abchurch Lane, London, demande les Médailles ci-dessous décrites :—

Nota.—Les Numéros renvoyent à la "List of Printers' Medals and Jettons," par M. Blades, 8vo., London, 1869.

Page. Pl.
1. A. *Av.* Busto d' "Aldus Pius Manutius."
2. B. *Av.* Buste de " Ioh. Petroius, Typographus."
5. F. *Av.* Busto de " Georg. Bawman, Typographus."
6. H. *Av.* Zacharias Roman.
    Rev. "Hedon my morghendy 1631."
10. N. *Av.* Minorve. "Acad. Lvgd. Batav."
    Rev. "Abrahamvs Elscvirivs 1652."
16. T. *Av.* Buste de I. A. Vulpius.
    Rev. "Gaudet Verona," &c., 1737.

Le Jubilé de 1740.

17. V. Altdorf.
    X. Anspach.
18. Y. Basle (Augst).
    Av. Mercure. Une presse typographique. Rerum tutissima Custos.
    Rev. Inscription seulement : " Artis Typogr.," &c.
20. 2A. Dresden.
    Av. "Mein eintzger Schein."
    "Dringt vielmahl ein."
    Rev. "Gottes Segen und Gedeyen"
    "Wird uns fernerweit erfreuen."
20. 2B. Erfurt.
    Av. Buste de Gutenberg sur un piédestal. Quatre livres avec leurs titres : "Digna Viro," &c.
    Rev. Minerve et la Typographie, le bouclier et le hibou : " Felici Fœdere," &c. Werner fecit Erford.
22. 2C. Gotha.
    Av. "Ut Aurora Musis amica Solem, &c.
23. 2D. *Av.* Inscription de 12 lignes commençant "Memor. fel. Jo. Guttenberg" et finissant : "Acre Modico Parara."
    Reb. Armoiries de la famille de Guttenberg. "Dissimulare hunc Virum &c.
27. 2G. Haarlem. Le "Grand Marsboorn."

Page. Pl.
38. 2P. Nuremberg.
Av. Un Vieillard dans les nuages. Minerve avec un phylactère. Quatre génies avec des instruments typographiques. " Gloria Germanorum &c.
Rev. Inscription : " D. G. Iubilæum Tertium " &c.
41. 2R. Ratisbonne.
Av. Armoires de la Ville. " Decus urbis et artis."
Rev. " Sacra dei bonori."

49. 3C. Grass et Barth, Breslau, 1804.
Av. Un Lion, un Aigle, 1504.
Rev. " Dreihundertiahriges," &c.
61. 3Q. Un jetton octogone de P. Dupont et Cie., 1836 ?
66. 3X. Un jetton, " Fonderie générale de caractères française et étrangère, 1837."
67. 3Y. Un jetton octogone de Lange Lévy et Cie., 1837.
68. 3Z. Turin.
Av. Buste de " Carolo Boucherono," J. Pomba, Typ., 1837.

Le Jubilé de 1840.

78. 4K. Francfort.
Av. Le monument des trois imprimeurs.
Rev. " Zu ehren," &c.
85. 4Q. Médaille des " Bibliopolæ et Typographi Lugdun."
86. 4R. Jetton de la " Société des Imprimeurs, Lyon."
89. 4V. Mayence ?
Av. Un livre. " Das erste buch."
Rev. " Erinnerung an die," &c.
91. 4Y. Paris. Médaille de Montagny. Les bustes de Gutenberg et Senefelder.

92. 4Z. Jetton pour la " Chambre des Imprimeurs " de Paris.
93. 5A. Jetton pour la " Conférence des Imprimeurs " de Paris.
109. 5Q. Amsterdam, 1857. " Typogr. Vereen. de Nederl. Drukpers.
112. 5V. Paris. Société pour la poursuite des contrefaçons.
113. 5Y. Paris. Société pour la défense de la propriété litt.
114. 5Y. Jetton A. Chaix et Cie. " Cours des apprentis."
117. 6B. Jetton Paul Dupont. Société de secours mutuel.

Cette Liste est destinée d'être détachée de la touche, et l'auteur prie avec instances de la faire circuler parmi les Imprimeurs, les Numismates, et les Amateurs.

DESIDERATA.

M. BLADES, 11, Abchurch Lane, London, demande les Médailles ci-dessous décrites:—

Nota.—Les Numéros renvoyent à la "List of Printers' Medals and Jettons," par M. Blades, 8vo., London, 1869.

Page. Pl.
1. A. *Av.* Buste d' "Aldus Pius Manutius."
2. B. *Av.* Buste de "Ioh. Petreius, Typographus."
5. F. *Av.* Buste de l' "Georg. Bawman, Typographus."
6. H. *Av.* Zacharias Roman.
   Rev. "Hedon my morghen dy 1631."
10. N. *Av.* Minerve. "Acad. Lvgd. Batav."
    Rev. "Abrahamvs Elsevirivs 1652."
16. T. *Av.* Buste de I. A. Vulpius.
    Rev. "Gaudet Verona," &c., 1737.

Le Jubilé de 1740.

17. V. Altdorf.
    X. Anspach.
18. Y. Basle (Augst).
    Av. Mercure. Une presse typographique. "Rerum tutissima Custos."
    Rev. Inscription seulement: "Artis Typogr.," &c.
20. 2A. Dresden.
    Av. "Mein einziger Schein."
    "Dringt vielmal ein."
    Rev. "Gottes Segen und Gedeyen"
    "Wird uns ferner weit erfreuen."
20. 2B. Erfurt.
    Av. Buste de Gutenberg sur un piédestal. Quatre livres avec leurs titres: "Digna Viro," &c.
    Rev. Minerve et la Typographie, le bouclier et le hibou: "Felici Foedere," &c. Werner fecit Erford.
22. 2C. Gotha.
    Av. "Ut Aurora Musis amica Solem, &c.
23. 2D. *Av.* Inscription de 12 lignes commençant "Moemor... Jo. Guttenberg" et finissant: "Aere Modico Papare."
    Rev. Armoiries de la famille de Guttenberg. "Dissimulare hunc Virum &c."
27. 2G. Haarlem. Le "Grand Marshoorn."

Page. Pl.
38. 2P. Nuremberg.
 Av. Un Vieillard dans les nuages. Minerve avec un phylactère. Quatre génies avec des instruments typographiques. "Gloria Germanorum" &c.
 Rev. Inscription: "D. G. Iubilæum Tertium" &c.

41. 2R. Ratisbonne.
 Av. Armoires de la Ville. "Decus urbis et artis."
 Rev. "Sacra dei honori."

49. 3C. Grass et Barth, Breslau, 1804.
 Av. Un Lion, un Aigle, 1504.
 Rev. "Dreihundertjahriges," &c.

61. 3Q. Un jetton octogone de P. Dupont et Cie., 1836 ?

66. 3X. Un jetton, "Fonderie générale de caractères française et étrangère, 1837."

67. 3Y. Un jetton octogone de Lange Lévy et Cie., 1837.

68. 3Z. Turin.
 Av. Buste de "Carolo Boncherono," J. Pomba, Typ., 1837.

Le Jubilé de 1840.

78. 4K. Francfort.
 Av. Le monument des trois imprimeurs.
 Rev. "Zu ehren," &c.

85. 4Q. Médaille des f" Bibliopolæ et Typographi Lugduni."

86. 4R. Jetton de la "Société des Imprimeurs, Lyon."

89. 4V. Mayence ?
 Av. Un livre. "Das erste buch."
 Rev. "Erinnerung an die," &c.

91. 4Y. Paris. Médaille de Montagny. Les bustes de Gutenberg et Senefelder.

92. 4Z. Jetton pour la "Chambre des Imprimeurs" de Paris.

93. 5A. Jetton pour la "Conférence des Imprimeurs" de Paris.

109. 5Q. Amsterdam, 1857. "Typogr. Vereen, de Nederl. Drukpers."

112. 5V. Paris. Société pour la poursuite des contrefaçons.

113. 5Y. Paris. Société pour la défense de la propriété litt.

114. 5Y. Jetton A. Chaix et Cie. "Cours des apprentis."

117. 6B. Jetton Paul Dupont. Société de secours mutuel.

www.ingramcontent.com/pod-product-compliance
Lightning Source LLC
Chambersburg PA
CBHW031851220426
43663CB00006B/576